TAKE
CONTROL
of OCD

TAKE CONTROL of OCD

Second Edition

A KID'S GUIDE to Conquering Anxiety and Managing OCD

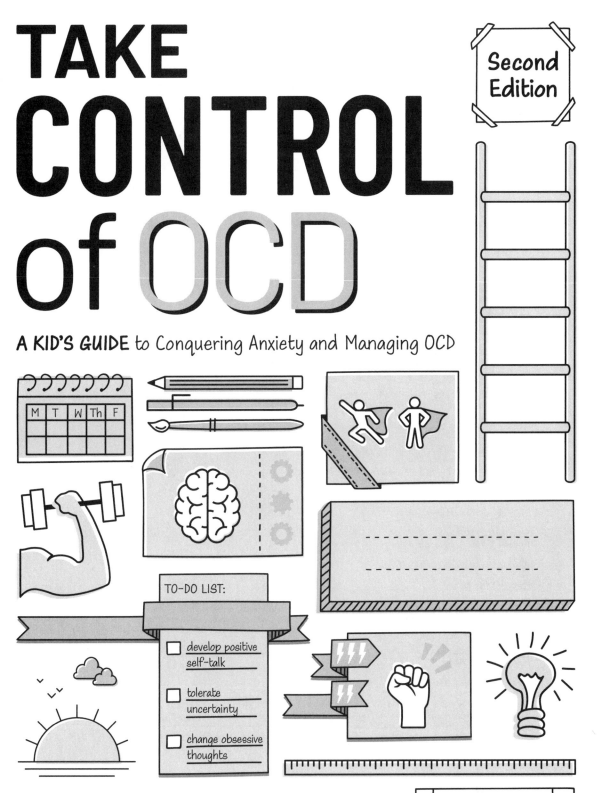

Bonnie Zucker, Psy.D.

PRUFROCK PRESS INC.
WACO, TEXAS

Library of Congress Cataloging-in-Publication Data

Names: Zucker, Bonnie, 1974- author.
Title: Take control of OCD: a kid's guide to conquering anxiety and
   managing ocd / Bonnie Zucker, Psy.D.
Description: 2nd ed. | Waco, TX : Prufrock Press Inc., 2021. | Includes
   bibliographical references. | Audience: Ages 10-16 | Summary: "Take
   Control of OCD: A Kid's Guide to Conquering Anxiety and Managing OCD" is
   a must-have guide for kids and teens ages 10-16 with
   Obsessive-Compulsive Disorder to help them take control and use their
   strengths to find success in school and in life"-- Provided by
   publisher.
Identifiers: LCCN 2021001109 (print) | LCCN 2021001110 (ebook) | ISBN
   9781646321193 (paperback) | ISBN 9781646321209 (ebook) | ISBN
   9781646321216 (epub)
Subjects: LCSH: Obsessive-compulsive disorder in children--Juvenile
   literature.
Classification: LCC RJ506.O25 Z83 2021 (print) | LCC RJ506.O25 (ebook) |
   DDC 618.92/85227--dc23
LC record available at https://lccn.loc.gov/2021001109
LC ebook record available at https://lccn.loc.gov/2021001110

Edited by Katy McDowall
Editorial Assistant: Andilynn Feddeler

Cover and layout design by Allegra Denbo

ISBN-13: 978-1-64632-119-3

Printed in the United States of America.

At the time of this book's publication, all facts and figures cited are the most current available. All telephone numbers, addresses, and website URLs are accurate and active. All publications, organizations, websites, and other resources exist as described in the book, and all have been verified. The authors and Prufrock Press Inc. make no warranty or guarantee concerning the information and materials given out by organizations or content found at websites, and we are not responsible for any changes that occur after this book's publication. If you find an error, please contact Prufrock Press Inc.

Prufrock Press Inc.
P.O. Box 8813
Waco, TX 76714-8813
Phone: (800) 998-2208
Fax: (800) 240-0333
https://www.prufrock.com

Dedication

For Brian and our sweet boys, Isaac and Todd, the
three greatest sources of love and joy that I have ever known.

Table of Contents

Acknowledgements

It is my privilege to be a therapist to so many extraordinary children and adults who have opened their worlds to me, sharing their struggles and trusting me to guide them well. This privilege is most pronounced in my work with children and adults with OCD. It is not easy to share one's most unwanted, most fearful thoughts, particularly those that call the self into question. For me to be on this journey with them, I am honored and extremely grateful. Week after week, their dedication to their psychological well-being and perseverance in facing their fears show their inner strength and truest resilience.

I have had the good fortune to have truly excellent teachers who have not only contributed to my knowledge, but also inspired an inner awareness that has been key to my success. Dr. Rudy Bauer has been of profound influence in my life and has taught me more about psyche and the mind than words could express. Thank you to Drs. Bernard Vittone and Mary Alvord, whose unwavering confidence in me from the beginning has been a treasured gift that has influenced me as a clinician in immeasurable ways. In addition, Dr. Vittone's assistance on the medication portion of this book was a tremendous help! A special thank-you to Dr. Lance Clawson for teaching me so much about the role of medication and supplements that have proven invaluable for so many. I would not be a psychologist if it weren't for Dr. Harvey Parker's kind heart and meaningful, ongoing presence in my life. Finally, I would not be nearly as good a psychologist if it weren't for Dr. John McPherrin's guidance and permission to be truly authentic.

Thank you to Dr. Judith Rapoport, who so generously agreed to review this book! Her contributions to the treatment of childhood obsessive-compulsive disorder are monumental. A special thank-you to Dr. Adrian Wells for his willingness to review the portions of the book on metacognitive therapy.

Katy McDowall's editorial excellence (and Lacy Compton's outstanding guidance on the first edition) has been invaluable in the process of writing this book.

My family and friends have been a constant source of support. Paramount among them is my husband, Brian. His support of my work and understanding of my passion for it are invaluable, and I am forever grateful for his love, sensitivity, and patience.

My mother was always there for me, unconditionally, providing so much love and unfailing support. Her early teachings of compassion and the importance of having direction and determination shaped my path in life. The first edition of this book was the second book I had written, and I will always be grateful that I got to see how proud it made her. My sisterhood and best friendship with Emily means more to me than words could say; I thank her for her wisdom, encouragement, and love. Finally, I thank my sister-in-law, Lisa, for her constant support of and genuine enthusiasm for all that I do.

A Note for Parents
(Have your parents read this!)

Congratulations on having your child read this book! Witnessing your child's struggle with OCD can be heartbreaking, frustrating, and anxiety-provoking for you. In addition, failed attempts at helping your child cope with this problem likely leave you with a deep sense of hopelessness. It is a huge challenge to watch your child suffer from OCD (and many families deal with it for years before getting help). Perhaps even more challenging are the constant accommodations that you make to try to help them feel more secure and comfortable. Warm, loving, well-intentioned parents find themselves bending over backward to help their child avoid OCD-inducing situations. Yet these attempts only end up reinforcing the OCD, making it stronger.

Well, there is hope! This book is your hope. Based on empirically supported treatment strategies, this book uses the cognitive-behavioral therapy (CBT) approach to guide your child through the process of taking control of OCD. Step by step, your child will learn how to understand their OCD and how it influences their life, identify its triggers, develop a hierarchy (ladder) to use in facing their fears, learn relaxation and stress management strategies, and discover how to challenge obsessive thoughts and repetitive worries through learning different techniques, including the invaluable method of making loop recordings. Most importantly, your child will learn to gradually face their fears and prevent themselves from engaging in rituals/compulsions that were used to reduce the anxiety stemming from the obsessive thoughts or images. This is called exposure/response prevention (ERP). Your child will learn how to cope with the anxiety that comes from having OCD, practice mindfulness, tolerate uncertainty, and push themselves to stay outside of their comfort zone. Finally, they will learn stress management techniques and relapse prevention tips.

I encourage you to take a look at this book either before or while your child is reading it, so that you can become familiar with the treatment approach and understand the strategies that they will learn. This way, you can cue them to use the strategies when they are triggered. (Alternatively, note that I also wrote a book specifically for parents called *Parenting Kids With OCD* that you may find useful.) I also want to mention that here in this updated edition, I have added many more examples of children and teens with OCD. I wanted to make it very likely that your child will find themselves in one of these examples, increasing their sense of feeling understood and not alone (if there is a "type" to their OCD symptoms, it will be less pathologizing and more comforting to know that it's not them, but instead the OCD, that is the problem).

Over the years, research has discovered, and I have treated, many types and presentations of OCD, including those that focus on some topics that you or your child may find sensitive and difficult to discuss, yet they are important to cover. These include OCD presentations regarding unwanted sexual thoughts that children experience as inappropriate, intrusive worries about sexual orientation that individuals experience (regardless of sexual orientation and how they identify), and fears about harming a younger child in a sexual way that individuals experience (though they are not pedophiles and will not act on these thoughts). Given that a good number of children and teens have these presentations of OCD, I have included these examples in the book. Please also note that OCD doubts that focus on sexual orientation arise differently than the typical struggle that many children and teens without OCD or with other types of OCD experience, that is, the notion of questioning or being unsure about one's sexual orientation. With sexual orientation type OCD, the thoughts are experienced as unwanted and intrusive, and they often lead to rumination and compulsions, such as checking or reassurance-seeking, unlike the typical questioning which usually does not create these symptoms.

It is important to point out that just by reading about each different type of OCD, it will not cause your child to develop that form of OCD. Although your child may not have heard of or be familiar with some of these sensitive topics, the benefit of including these examples for those children and teens who struggle with these OCD themes outweighs the risks of hearing about these concepts for those who do not. Therefore, they are included in the book (and for most readers, their focus will be exclusively on their own type of OCD anyway). At the root of OCD are intrusive, unwanted thoughts (obsessions) that create a strong sense of self-doubt. The specific presentation of OCD varies from person to person, and although the content of their particular OCD matters to them, from a treatment perspective, the content is actually not relevant. Rather, it's about changing their relationship with the OCD thoughts and learning to tolerate uncertainty.

Throughout the process, your child is encouraged to request and receive support from you and possibly others they trust. The best advice I have is to meet your child where they are, respect their process for working through this program, and support them in any effort they make. Show compassion for how hard it is to be working on their OCD and praise them for all the effort it takes. You may be asked to participate in the "exposure" phase when they face their fears and practice previously avoided situations. Offering your presence, help with making the exposures happen, and on-the-spot encouragement will be valuable gifts for your child. Finally, make sure to congratulate your child and celebrate their progress along the way!

Best wishes,

Dr. Bonnie Zucker

Introduction
How to Use This Book

Let me start by congratulating you for picking up this book. By starting this book today, you are making a very smart decision—**to take control of OCD**! If you have obsessive-compulsive disorder (OCD), you know the hold it has had on your life, how it has influenced you, and surely, at times, how it has made things very difficult for you. Reading this book is a huge step in the direction of stopping the OCD from running your life, and by using the strategies here, you will gain the freedom you want and deserve!

To be clear, the fact that you have been suffering all of this time does not mean that you haven't tried to stop the OCD. In fact, trying but not being able to get rid of the OCD is part of having the disorder. And it's not your fault that you have it. Having OCD doesn't mean that there is anything wrong with you or that you aren't normal, and it doesn't mean that you can't live a great life. It has nothing to do with how capable you are, how successful you are or will be, or how smart you are (in fact, most people with OCD are very bright thinkers). Having OCD only means that you have OCD.

By deciding to start this book and investing the time and effort in the program described here, you are on your way to feeling better. The book is divided into 12 chapters, and you should read them in order and do the work that is involved. For example, Chapter 3 is called Developing Your Ladder and asks that you make a list of all of the things that are hard for you to do and that you avoid doing because of OCD. Making this ladder (and actually writing all of the things on the steps of the ladder) is a necessary part of challenging the OCD. Making an actual ladder (on paper or poster board) will drastically improve your chances of having success in overcoming the OCD. So, reading the chapters and doing the work is key! It might feel like a lot of work to do, but keep in mind that the OCD itself takes a lot of work—it is time-consuming and interferes with your life. It's better to do the work in this book than to do the work that OCD requires. Just take it one step, or one chapter, at a time.

The first chapter describes OCD, lists common obsessions and compulsions, and introduces many examples; Chapter 2 explains how to overcome OCD; Chapter 3 is about making your ladder; Chapter 4 teaches you relaxation strategies; Chapter 5 is about challenging the thoughts and worries related to the OCD; Chapter 6 is the second part of challenging the thoughts related to OCD and teaches you how to do loop and imaginal exposure recordings; Chapter 7 explains how to deal with uncertainty; Chapter 8 addresses other conditions that may occur at the same time as OCD; Chapters 9 and 10 teach you how to face your fears through "exposure"; Chapter 11 discusses how to manage stress; and finally, Chapter 12 is a celebration of your hard work and gives you ideas about how to deal with OCD symptoms if they come up again.

Many readers will find it helpful to ask their parents for help when using this book, and others will want to keep it to themselves. Either way will work, and it's just a matter of what feels right to you.

Throughout the book, I will describe examples of kids with OCD. These are descriptions of children I have worked with over the years, but their names and identifying information have been changed to protect their privacy.

Even though I haven't met you in person, I want you to know that I am extremely proud of you for reading this book and for doing the work you are about to do. It won't always be super easy, but if you stick with it (even through the sticky parts), you will come out on top! You will feel better, and **you will take control of OCD**!

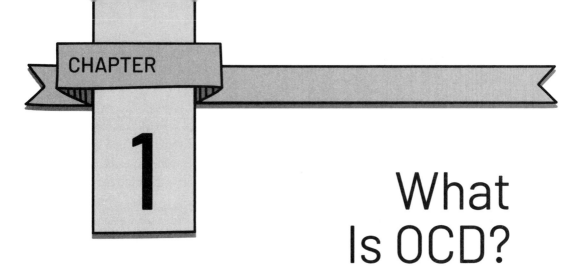

What Is OCD?

"I never really liked things like sharing drinks or using bathrooms in the mall. But about a year ago, it really became a problem for me. I couldn't stop thinking about being contaminated and all the things I touched and who I was near. At first, the rituals were small and not a big deal—I would just wash one more time or ask one little question to check if someone was not sick. Over time, however, they became more detailed and involved, and took much longer. Eventually, it felt like most of my time was spent either thinking about these fears or doing something to try to make them better, like washing again and again and moving seats if someone at the table had been sick."

—Andrew, age 12

OCD stands for obsessive-compulsive disorder, and it is characterized by having the same thought, urge, or image over and over, which is called an "obsession." An obsession is usually followed by some repetitive behavior, ritual, or mental action (things you do in your mind like counting), which is called a "compulsion." To have OCD, you have to have either obsessions or compulsions, but most people have both. Compulsions are usually done to make the obsessions better. Obsessions are unwanted and feel intrusive, meaning that they interfere with whatever you are doing, and they are repetitive, meaning that they occur over and over. Obsessions usually cause a feeling of anxiety or distress. Compulsions also tend to be repetitive, and the person does the behavior or ritual again and again, usually to try to feel better about the obsessions or lessen the bad feelings that come from having them. For example, a classic type of OCD is "contamination" type, where you may touch a bathroom door handle and begin to think obsessively about germs or being infected with an illness (this is the "obsession"). These thoughts occur again and again and cause you to feel very worried and uncomfortable. Then, as a way of dealing with the repetitive and disturbing thoughts and anxiety about germs, you wash your hands several times. Washing your hands is the "compulsive" behavior, or ritual, that you do to try to get rid of the germs (and the thoughts about the germs). Usually, the washing is excessive, meaning that you will wash for a long time and will rewash your hands. The problem is that the handwashing becomes a repetitive behavior (something you do again and again) and only works to get rid of the obsessive thoughts for the short term. In the long term, the OCD is becoming stronger.

> **obsessions:** thoughts, ideas, images, or urges
>
> **compulsions:** behaviors, rituals, or mental actions

A symptom is a sign that something is wrong. For instance, sneezing and coughing are symptoms of a cold. Similarly, obsessions and compulsions are symptoms of OCD. To be "diagnosed" with OCD, you need to have either obsessions or compulsions, or both. The obsessions and compulsions need to make you feel distressed (very upset), need to take more than 1 hour a day, and need to interfere with your normal activities like school, social activities, or relationships with others. Because the symptoms of OCD are distracting, it can be hard to concentrate on things like schoolwork or having fun at social events. Because the symptoms of OCD are time-consuming, it can be hard to spend time with friends and family in a normal way and be on time to places like school.

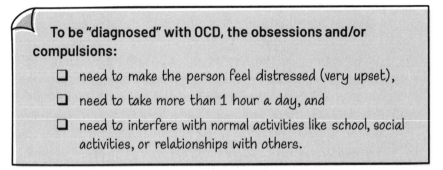

To be "diagnosed" with OCD, the obsessions and/or compulsions:

☐ need to make the person feel distressed (very upset),

☐ need to take more than 1 hour a day, and

☐ need to interfere with normal activities like school, social activities, or relationships with others.

Obsessions are not just regular worries about real-life situations like having a project due for school or having an argument with a friend. Instead, obsessions are usually about unrealistic or impossible threats (for example, getting cancer from bathrooms, being punished by God), or they are exaggerated fears about actual but unlikely threats (for example, eating contaminated food). About 1%–4% of children and teens have OCD. There is also a strong relationship between childhood and adulthood OCD, meaning that if it isn't addressed and treated when you're young, it will likely continue when you're an adult. There are also many other children and teens with anxiety disorders who have some obsessive-compulsive symptoms without having full OCD. When this happens, we call it "obsessive-compulsive features."

Keep in mind that OCD creates a sense of self-doubt (and doubt in general) and can invade any aspect of life. Often, someone with OCD will have unwanted, intrusive thoughts about areas of life that could feel vulnerable. You will see in the following list that OCD can affect the way you feel about family members, make you question if you are good or not, create doubt around your sexual orientation, or even make you worry that you would do something bad to someone else. Although each person with OCD will experience different symptoms, there are many common themes and types of obsessions and compulsions. I have included a very long list here, with the goal that you can find your particular type. However, if you don't see your type listed, do not be discouraged, as OCD can manifest in many different ways.

Types of OCD Presentations

> **Contamination OCD:** Thinking about being infected with germs, diseases, and dirt from touching surfaces, other people, or things, or from eating certain foods.

> **Mental contamination OCD:** When you feel that you are contaminated by just thinking about or imagining a situation or a person who is contaminated. For example, this usually involves a person who has hurt you (such as a bully), and just thinking of them makes you feel like washing yourself. Mental contamination often involves feeling dirty even though you have not come into contact with a contaminated person or object.

> **Emotional contamination OCD:** When you fear that you could become like somebody or begin to have their negative qualities or personality traits. This could come up around people with physical or intellectual disabilities, and when this happens, you may be afraid that you will "catch" the disability. With this type of OCD, it is not necessary to come in close contact with the "contaminated" person. Instead, it could just be from seeing them from afar or even just thinking about them. It can also come as worry that you might start to have the same thoughts and feelings that someone else is having. The fear could also be about someone else "stealing" your qualities or personality traits, such as "stealing my smarts." It could also be less specific, for example, walking by a garbage can and worrying about becoming a waste collector.

> **Doubting OCD:** Wondering if you did or didn't do something like leave a door unlocked or if you remembered to bring something with you.

> **Indecisive OCD:** Questioning if you made the right choice or not being able to make a decision, even to the point where you might miss a deadline. Even after the decision is made, you continue to question if it was the right choice.

> **Checking OCD:** Repetitive thoughts about leaving something on, like the oven, or forgetting personal items. You may experience urges to check an outlet or candle, even when they were not used recently.

> **Symmetry OCD:** Needing things to be in a certain order or doing things in a way that feels correct to you.

> **"Just feels right" OCD:** Getting stuck on something because it doesn't "feel right" to you, such as feeling that the way you touched the table wasn't the "right" way or feeling like the word you said wasn't the "right" word to use. Often without it even being specific, there is a feeling that things are not right when things are not a certain way.

> **Scrupulosity OCD:** Having religious or moral doubt; experiencing disturbing sexual thoughts or urges.

> **"Bad" thoughts OCD:** This is when the intrusive thoughts focus on bad or violent things happening to you or someone you care about. It often involves violent thoughts or images.

> **Harm OCD:** Fear of doing harm to someone, either purposely or by doing something unintentional that may put others at risk.

> **Sexual OCD:** When you have intrusive, inappropriate sexual thoughts. It could include unwanted thoughts about being sexual with relatives or others with whom it would be inappropriate to be sexual.

> **Pedophilia OCD:** When you worry that you are a pedophile and worry that you could or would harm a child or touch children in a sexual way. (*Note*: It's important to know that these thoughts are not desires, meaning that you don't want to act on your thoughts, and that these thoughts are very upsetting, distressing, and embarrassing to talk about.)

> **Sexual orientation OCD:** This is when you have excessive worries related to your sexual orientation. People with sexual orientation OCD may constantly question their sexuality or obsessively worry about how they identify, regardless of their sexual orientation, and they often seek reassurance from others that they identify in a specific way (e.g., heterosexual, gay, etc.). (*Note*: It's important to know that the worries associated with this type of OCD do not mean that you are homoprejudiced or have anything against any form of sexual orientation.)

> **Relationship OCD:** Although this type is usually seen in adults, it can begin in teenage years. This is when you are in a romantic relationship and constantly question how you feel about your partner or how they feel about you, and when you have trouble tolerating the uncertainty of not knowing if the relationship is a good one or will work out.

> **Pure-O OCD:** This is when the OCD is mostly thoughts without doing any obvious behaviors, rituals, or compulsions. Most of the time, however, this type does involve a mental compulsion.

> **Hypochondria/Health OCD:** When the obsessive thoughts focus on getting sick, having an illness (usually significant, such as cancer), or having something wrong health-wise.
> **"Need to confess" OCD:** This is when you feel like you have to "confess" or share (often with a parent) something that you did or may have done that you worry is bad to have done (for example, if you worry that you have "sinned"). It could also be a general feeling of needing to report your actions as a way of checking that you did everything right, or correctly.
> **Somatic/Hyperawareness OCD:** This is when you are hyper-focused on a body part or body function, such as breathing or blinking. Persistent thoughts about the part interfere with your ability to focus on other things and bring all the attention to scanning and focusing on that part of the body. It's not about wanting to change the part or the sensation; it's about being aware of it all the time.
> **Olfactory OCD:** This is when you have excessive thoughts about smelling bad and believe others smell your odor. Those with olfactory OCD often report detecting unpleasant smells.

Types of Compulsions

> Washing/cleaning
> Checking
> Scanning for danger and things that could be risky or harmful
> Counting
> Ordering/arranging/straightening
> Touching things in a certain way or a certain number of times
> Doing things in evens or odds
> Walking in a certain way, either in a pattern or avoiding lines or cracks
> Repeating actions
> Shaking your head or doing other movements to "undo" bad thoughts or images
> Waiting until it "feels right" or doing it over until it feels right
> Praying, asking God for forgiveness
> Driving back to check if you ran over something
> Asking for reassurance (for example, asking others to tell you it will be okay)
> Avoiding making a decision or letting others decide for you
> Avoiding being near younger children or alone with younger children

> Avoiding sitting in the same seat that someone else sat in
> Avoiding people or situations that trigger your OCD
> Avoiding people of the same gender for fears that you might be gay, lesbian, or bisexual (regardless of how you identify)
> Seeking constant reassurance that you do not present as a particular sexual orientation
> Questioning your feelings for the person you are in a relationship with
> Checking to see if you have feelings for other people, comparing them to your current romantic partner
> Hoarding (saving a great amount of stuff and refusing to get rid of any of it)
> Seeking medical attention to reduce worries about health concerns
> Scanning your body for health-related symptoms
> Needing to ask/tell/confess
> Continually focusing on physical sensations
> Scanning others to see if they look repulsed by how you smell
> Showering multiple times a day to ensure that you don't smell

Common OCD Thinking Patterns and Beliefs

There are certain thinking patterns and beliefs that are commonly seen in people with OCD, and it is useful to identify which ones are relevant to you, as this will help you to better understand what thoughts are coming from OCD and how to challenge them. Many of these thinking patterns have to do with how you think about your thoughts and with what you think will happen if you think a certain way or think about certain things.

Overestimation of Danger

People with OCD tend to overestimate the risk of danger and believe that the world is threatening and dangerous. There is an exaggerated sense that something bad will happen or go wrong, and as a result, they believe certain things need to be done to prevent harm and to keep themselves and their loved ones safe. Often included in this belief is the idea that making mistakes and doing something wrong will lead to bad outcomes and responsibility for those outcomes. For example, Andrew thought it was easy to get sick from using public bathrooms, so he labeled them as very dangerous and unsafe. He thought that if he didn't wash his hands thoroughly enough, he would be to blame for getting sick and for getting others sick as well. Sydney thought that it was easy to step on an animal and kill it and that walking outside was dangerous. Her worry about hurting or killing an animal was very strong.

Desire for Certainty

Many individuals with OCD want to know *for sure* that something did or did not happen. Often, it's about making sure that something bad didn't happen or won't happen. This leads to a lot of doubting, checking, and asking behaviors in search of certainty. For example, Alicia wanted absolute certainty that her milk was safe and unspoiled, and the expiration date wasn't good enough—she even doubted that it was correct.

Perfectionism

Perfectionism is the belief that things should be perfect and that they aren't right or correct unless they are perfect. Not only does the individual believe it is *possible* to be perfect, or to do things perfectly, but also they are not comfortable and things don't feel right unless they are considered to be perfect. This belief often results in ordering, checking, redoing tasks, rewriting, and so on. For example, Jasmine couldn't relax when in her bed unless the blanket was perfectly flat, straight, and evenly distributed on the bed. She also had a hard time working at her desk unless everything was perfectly aligned. Perfectionism can also come out as a need for completeness, like having a complete understanding of something, or needing to be complete when explaining something. For example, a 13-year-old client named Katherine needed to provide every detail when explaining something to the point that her parents had to listen for 45 minutes as she explained the details of her school day.

Rigid/Moral-Themed Thinking

Some kids with OCD, like William, have rigid thinking that is grounded in moral or religious ideals. This type of thinking assumes that there is a fundamental right and wrong and that a person can be punished by God or go to heaven or hell based on how they think or behave. This usually results in a rigid way of behaving and living based on the fear of being punished or doomed. The person ends up doubting their own true self and that they are a good person at the core. Other forms of moral thinking are focused on being "good" or doing things ethically, without religion tied in. Children with this belief may judge others harshly for breaking the rules or doing things they shouldn't be doing. Although breaking the rules is not ideal, the problem here is the intensity of judgment and rigidity.

Overimportance of Thoughts

In OCD, thoughts have a lot of meaning associated with them, and there often are faulty beliefs linked to the thoughts. Thoughts are considered to be as powerful as actions or events. This pattern of thinking magnifies the power of thoughts and makes it feel like thoughts are the same as actions or mean as much as actions do. This is similar to a fusion belief (see Chapter 5), which is the belief that having a thought about something bad happening means that it will happen. Similarly, thoughts are considered to be true and accurate representations of what you really feel or want, which leads to doubting who you are and what you feel. In other words, there is no boundary between thinking about doing something and actually doing it.

Overresponsibility

This is when there is a strong sense of feeling responsible and making sure that something bad doesn't happen or others don't get hurt. This usually leads to a lot of checking and taking preventative steps to decrease the chances of something bad happening. Checking all of the outlets, stove, and oven, and turning all of the lights off before leaving the house is an example of overresponsibility.

A Summary of Thinking Patterns and Beliefs

Children and teens with OCD usually feel strongly driven to do the compulsive behaviors and feel that they cannot control the urge to do the behaviors. Although compulsions are usually done to lessen the distress caused by the obsession, they also can be done because the person thinks that doing them will prevent something bad from happening (for example, walking in a certain way to protect someone you love). Sometimes, compulsions involve rigid or stereotyped actions that are completed according to self-created, very detailed rules (for example, ordering your books from shortest to tallest in a very specific order while saying the alphabet). Most people have a hard time explaining *why* they are doing the compulsions. They often know that the compulsions don't make sense, but the urge to do them is very, very strong.

Originally, OCD was considered to be an anxiety disorder. The most recent categorization, however, put OCD in its own category (along with other disorders such as hair-pulling disorder, called trichotillomania; see Chapter 8). Most children and teens with OCD have anxiety and get very activated from it, but it is not necessary to experience the obsessions or compulsions as anxiety-causing in order to have OCD.

OCD Cycle

Regardless of which type of OCD you have, OCD happens in a cycle. There is a pattern to how OCD gets triggered (meaning how it gets "set off"). Although sometimes it simply comes up out of the blue (for example, an idea just pops into your head and you get stuck on the thought), most often there is an order to how the OCD plays out:

1. event (trigger situation),
2. thought (obsession/obsessive thought or image),
3. feeling (anxiety, fear, discomfort), and then
4. action (compulsion/compulsive behavior).

Dr. Bruce Hyman and Cherry Pedrick (2010) explained it in a similar way:

1. "activating event,"
2. "unrealistic appraisal of event,"
3. "excessive anxiety," and then
4. "neutralizing ritual."

Take a look at the "OCD Cycle" graphic and the "OCD Cycle Example" graphic.

OCD Cycle

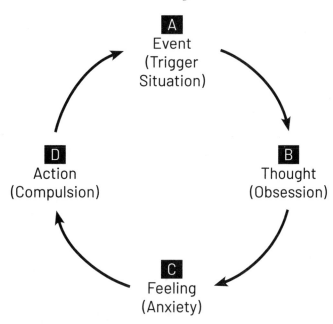

OCD Cycle Example

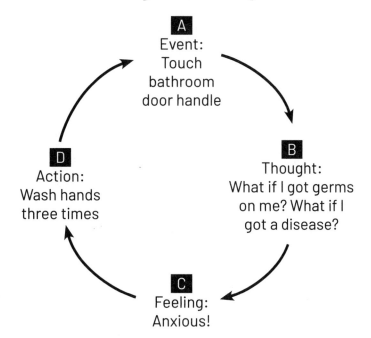

To make the OCD cycle clear, let's go through a few examples. Here are examples, going from simple to more complicated and involved.

EXAMPLE 1
Andrew, 12 years old, OCD: Contamination Type

Event: Use public bathroom.

Thought: I can't touch the toilet, flusher, faucets, or doorknob because there are dangerous germs on all of them. Maybe I touched someone's germs and will get sick.

Feeling: Very, very anxious!

Action: Wash hands and use paper towels to turn off faucet and open doorknob.

EXAMPLE 2
Alicia, 11 years old, OCD: Contamination Type

Event: Eat cookie from bake sale.

Thought: What if the person who baked it was sick? Now I will get their germs and be sick, too! The eggs could have salmonella in them, or the ingredients could be old and expired! What if I throw up?

Feeling: Very, very anxious!

Action: Ask Mom for reassurance that the cookies were safe. Ask friends if they ate cookies from the bake sale and see how they are feeling. Wait 3 days until I feel sure that I didn't get sick from bake sale cookies.

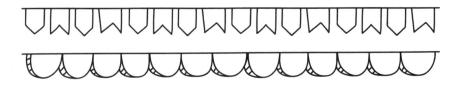

EXAMPLE 3

Tyler, 13 years old, OCD: Emotional Contamination Type

Event: Think about high school boy who committed suicide.

Thought: Why would he have killed himself? What was he thinking? What were his thoughts that made him commit suicide? What if I think about the thoughts he could have had and then I mistake them for my own thoughts and commit suicide also? What if no one knows that I didn't really mean to kill myself?

Feeling: Very, very anxious and scared!

Action: Ask for reassurance, "I'm not suicidal, right?" from parents. Avoid listening to a song that triggers those thoughts.

EXAMPLE 4

Sydney, 10 years old, OCD: Doubting/Indecisiveness Types

Event: Step on something.

Thought: What if I stepped on a bug and killed it?

Feeling: Very, very anxious!

Action: Go back and check sidewalk.

EXAMPLE 5

Connor, 16 years old, OCD: Harm Type

Event: Someone sneezes at school.

Thought: What if I am sick and I spread germs and get someone else sick? What if I have the flu? What if I spread it and someone dies?

Feeling: Very, very anxious!

Action: Keep distance from others, avoid lunchroom and eat alone in classroom instead, and use shirt to open doors. Avoid social plans for a few days to ensure I'm not really sick and don't have the flu.

EXAMPLE 6
William, 16 years old, OCD: Scrupulosity Type

Event: Asked to go to a party with friends.

Thought: I shouldn't have fun or else I will be punished. Something bad will happen if I enjoy myself and feel pleasure.

Feeling: Very, very anxious!

Action: Tell my friends that I can't go. Stay home and do homework instead.

EXAMPLE 7
Jasmine, 15 years old, OCD: Symmetry/"Just Feels Right" Types

Event: Look at desk.

Thought: Things are out of order. They need to be straight.

Feeling: Very, very uncomfortable!

Action: Order and arrange everything until it is all lined up.

EXAMPLE 8
Lina, 12 years old, OCD: Sexual Orientation Type

Event: Changing in girls' locker room for PE. A friend is talking to me while we are changing, so I look in her direction.

Thought: What if I'm really looking at her because I want to see her without a shirt? What if she sees me looking at her? What if I have feelings for her? What if I'm a lesbian?

Feeling: Very, very anxious!

Action: Keep the conversation short, look away, avoid talking to my friend for the rest of PE. Scan body for signs of attraction.

EXAMPLE 9

Kevin, 14 years old, OCD: Pedophilia Type

Event: Walk by a park with other kids playing.

Thought: What if I hurt one of those kids or touched their privates? What if someone knew my thoughts? Does thinking it mean that I did it? Is it as bad as doing it?

Feeling: Very, very anxious!

Action: Shake head four times to the right, quickly and forcefully.

EXAMPLE 10

Talia, 17 years old, OCD: Hypochondria/Health Type

Event: Heard about a girl who was diagnosed with leukemia.

Thought: What if I have leukemia? What if I die from it? What if the treatments don't work for me?

Feeling: Very, very anxious!

Action: Ask Mom for reassurance that she isn't sick. Request to see a doctor for bloodwork. Read about symptoms of leukemia in teens online. Read stories about teens who've been diagnosed with leukemia. Scan body for signs of illness.

In Chapter 3, we will go through these examples in more detail, and you will see the ladders that each of these children and teens used to face their OCD.

There also are individuals who have OCD that doesn't fit into one of the examples or doesn't follow the cycle I described. For example, there often can be an obsessive image that is not a thought. Eleven-year-old Mark would see lines all over the place when he walked into rooms. His mind just "saw" these connecting lines, and it was very hard for him to concentrate and think clearly because the lines he saw all over the place made it difficult for him to notice other things. Fifteen-year-old Ashley would get stuck on certain mathematical formulas, such as seeing two perpendicular lines, and would obsessively think about the point at which they connected/intersected and how that point was "double counted" in that it was part of two different lines. For both Mark and Ashley, their compulsions made them focus on and think about the lines and math formulas until they reached a point when it "felt right" or "felt okay," and then they could focus on something else. They did not have the "just feels right" type exactly, although the compulsion to think about certain things over and over until it did sit well with them appeared similar.

Causes of OCD

It is not completely clear what causes OCD, but it is clear that it involves certain parts of the brain working differently than they should. Although there is nothing wrong with the *structure* of the brain, there is miscommunication between some of the different parts. As a result, the brain sort of hiccups, and you end up getting stuck on the same thought—which is the OCD. Everyone has a part of their brain that is called the amygdala, and this is where the "fight-or-flight" response comes from. When you perceive a threat, your amygdala creates a response to be able to deal with the threat for survival. This part of the brain is separate from the other part of the brain that makes sense of things and uses reasoning skills (called the prefrontal cortex). This way, your brain doesn't need to make too much sense of the threat, or even figure out if it is a real threat or not, before it reacts to it with the fight-or-flight response. This is useful in some cases, like if a lion was running toward you. However, it is not useful when you are perceiving something that is not actually a threat (for example, touching a doorknob). It's useful to understand how the brain works, and also to know that even a thought can trigger a threat response. Just thinking of a something that feels threatening can trigger the amygdala to react.

Most researchers believe that OCD is something you are born with (meaning that it is genetic and runs in families) and that it simply comes out at a certain point as you are growing up. Because OCD symptoms worsen with stress, it also is important to consider that children who are born with the tendency to have OCD may have it come out during or after a period of high stress. Parents cannot cause OCD in their children out of the blue, but if their child has the genes for OCD in the first place, parents may do things that cause the OCD to come out. For example, it is possible that a child's parent has OCD and models OCD behaviors that the individual ends up learning to do as well. This is called "modeling," and when this happens, it is not because the parent meant to teach their child OCD behaviors. Also, parents who are very demanding and perfectionistic or overly critical or rigid with their children may increase the chances that their children will develop OCD. Although this is not done on purpose, it can contribute to the OCD coming out.

There is research that suggests that a small number of children may develop OCD (or their OCD may worsen) after having many strep infections or a certain form of strep throat. In these cases, the OCD symptoms come up suddenly and intensely. These less common cases of OCD are called PANDAS (pediatric autoimmune neuropsychiatric disorder associated with strep) and PANS (pediatric acute-onset neuropsychiatric syndrome), and they require typical OCD treatment (see Chapter 2). PANDAS and PANS are controversial, and the treatment for them is not well understood or supported by research. Although there is still more research needed on this topic, I caution you and your parents that there are professionals who quickly recommend extreme and aggressive treatments (including plasmapheresis and intravenous immunoglobulin therapy). In addition to following the program described in this book, it's best to work with a psychiatrist or other specialist who can explore a less extreme approach before considering these last-resort options.

OCD often comes up gradually, starting with an upsetting or unwanted thought or two, and then you may have begun to do a compulsive behavior or ritual here and there. When the compulsion relieves the unsettled feeling or anxiety that comes from the obsessions, it increases the chances that you will continue to do the compulsions once the obsessions come up again. Then, OCD starts to take more and more time, and suddenly, you or your parent(s) may see that it's interfering with your life in some way. Most of the time, children, teens, and their parents do not realize at first that it is OCD. It usually takes a while to figure it out.

Most of your characteristics—the color of your eyes, if math comes naturally or not, if you have allergies—are determined by your genes. You are born a certain way, and this cannot be changed. Nor would you want to change it because you are unique and were born with great characteristics. We don't want to change you! However, OCD is just like if you have allergies—you treat them by seeing a doctor and perhaps taking allergy medication, you make sure that your house is clean and not dusty, avoid certain foods, and so on. By doing these things, you end up not suffering from allergies. Similarly, by learning how to treat OCD, you will end up not suffering from it anymore.

This is the *good news*: OCD is very treatable, meaning that you can work through this program and overcome OCD. Research has shown that you can change how your brain works by training your brain to respond a different way. Our goal is to reprogram your brain so that you don't struggle with OCD anymore. It is your decision to overcome OCD, and it will be your hard work that will make this a success. It won't always be easy, but it will work. I've seen it work successfully with hundreds of kids and teens. You can do it!

What I Know Now

In this chapter, you learned the definition of OCD and the many types of OCD presentations and compulsions. You also learned about the different OCD beliefs. We reviewed the OCD cycle: **(1)** triggering event, **(2)** thought (obsession), **(3)** feeling (anxiety), and **(4)** action (compulsion, ritual), and we went through several examples to better understand how the cycle works. Then, you learned about the causes of OCD and how we can change how the brain works. Finally, you learned that by following this program, you can overcome OCD!

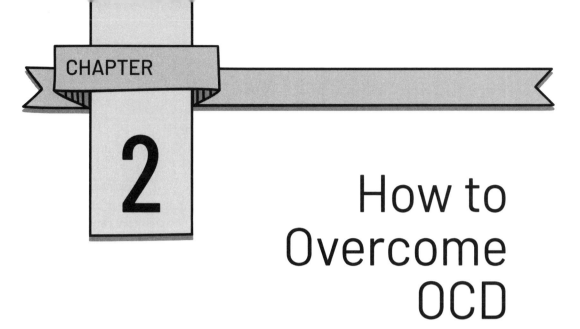

2

How to Overcome OCD

"OCD had taken a huge toll on my life and prevented me from living fully and completely. However, I found out that there are steps you can take to reduce your anxious symptoms and more fully enjoy life."

—William, age 16

Starting right now, I would like you to think differently about OCD. Instead of it being a part of you, I'd like you to begin thinking about it as something separate. You are you, and you have OCD. Let's look at it as YOU versus the OCD. This is called "externalizing the OCD." Because you've had OCD symptoms, they may have felt like they were a part of you or that because the OCD is coming from your brain, it means it's *you*. However, this is not correct. We want to start thinking of OCD as separate from who you are and as something you can challenge directly, just like if you were playing against someone in a sport or a game. You want to think about that other player and the moves they are going to make to learn how to have a good offense and defense. The more you understand how OCD works—how it tries to gain power over you, what it says to you to gain that power, and how it gets stronger in certain situations—the easier it will be to win against it! By better understanding how your OCD works—how it gets set off, or triggered, and how the compulsions feed into it, making it stronger—the clearer you will be on what to do to challenge it.

> **externalizing the OCD:** when you think about OCD as something separate, instead of it being a part of you; it's you versus OCD

The first step is to understand your symptoms and how OCD impacts your life—what behaviors you do and don't do in response to OCD, and what situations you avoid because of OCD (which we will make into a ladder). In the upcoming chapters, you will list the situations that you avoid, and this will set the stage for overcoming OCD. You also will learn how to identify when OCD is "talking to you" by making a list called "When my OCD talks, it says . . ."—this list will help you understand when OCD is trying to influence you. You will learn many strategies and techniques to overcome both the thoughts and behaviors of OCD and minimize its impact on your life. You will learn ways not to be "organized" by OCD, meaning that OCD won't influence how you do things and live your life. By challenging it head on, through exposure/response prevention (ERP), using loops, and possibly imaginal exposure recordings, all of which will be explained in detail in this and upcoming chapters, you will master this and come out on top!

Cognitive-Behavioral Therapy

The research on OCD shows that the best approach to treating it is cognitive-behavioral therapy (CBT). Although other types of therapy, such as acceptance and commitment therapy (ACT) and Internal Family Systems (IFS), have also been shown effective, the strongest results are associated with CBT.

CBT explains that OCD, similar to anxiety disorders, has three parts:
1. body,
2. thoughts, and
3. behavior.

When you are having OCD symptoms, it comes out in your body, thoughts, and behavior. Your **body** feels different when you are completely relaxed than it does when you are stuck on OCD thoughts, stressed out, worried, or scared. Obsessive thoughts, ideas, and worries are the **thoughts** part: You will worry, have certain thinking patterns, and think certain thoughts to yourself when you are focused on obsessions. Your actions or **behavior** will be different when you are stuck in the OCD cycle compared to when you are not. Most often, the behavior will be compulsions and rituals, but it can also be avoidance behaviors.

The following is a list of common body, thought, and behavioral symptoms related to OCD.

Common Body Symptoms

> Muscle tension
> Fast heartbeat
> Sweaty palms
> Shallow breathing
> Stomachaches
> Headaches
> Feeling dizzy or lightheaded
> Hot flashes
> Restless or panicky

Common Thought Symptoms

> Obsessive thoughts, ideas, or images
> Worries
> Thinking errors/mistakes
> Negative self-talk
> Doubting, questioning, ruminating

Common Behavioral Symptoms

> Compulsions/rituals (washing, checking, ordering, repeating, confessing)
> Avoidance of situations
> Nervous behaviors (asking for reassurance from others)

The "Body, Thoughts, Behavior" graphic is a diagram of the three parts, including descriptions of each part.

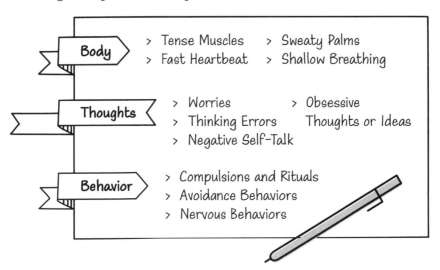

To treat OCD, we need to address all three parts: body, thoughts, and behavior. Chapter 4 is about relaxation, which deals with the body; Chapters 5 and 6 address the thoughts part; and Chapters 9 and 10 focus on changing your behavior. You will learn how to calm and relax your body, identify and challenge obsessive thinking patterns, become desensitized to and bored by obsessive thoughts, replace worried thoughts with realistic ones, master worries, talk back to OCD with positive self-talk, and experience your thoughts differently by learning mindfulness and similar techniques. You also will learn how to be comfortable with not having certainty, or not knowing *for sure*. You will be able to do this by learning "uncertainty training." To stop doing the compulsions, you will learn how to face your fears. Once you know the strategies, you will be ready to practice "exposing" yourself to the OCD situations and stop engaging in rituals and other compulsions. You will do this with exposure/response prevention (ERP).

The following is a summary of the strategies that you will learn.

Body

> Calm breathing
> One-nostril breathing
> Progressive muscle relaxation
> Relaxing imagery
> Mindfulness meditation
> Yoga

Thoughts

> "Stamping" it "OCD"
> Positive self-talk
> Distraction
> Identifying and challenging thinking errors
> Thought challenge form
> Detached mindfulness
> Attention training technique
> Worry and uncertainty training loops
> Imaginal exposure recordings

Behavior

> Create a ladder of anxiety-provoking situations
> Exposure/response prevention (ERP)
> Parents/family stop accommodating the OCD

Exposure/Response Prevention (ERP)

Exposure/response prevention (ERP) is the best way to overcome OCD because it involves practicing the situations that you avoid because of OCD and then not doing your typical response (usually a ritual).

> **exposure:** when you purposely practice being in an anxiety or trigger situation as a way of facing your fears

When you are exposed to the situations you avoid, this is called an "exposure." Doing an exposure is when you purposely practice being in a situation that triggers OCD as a way of facing your fears. For example, if you worry about being contaminated by germs and wash your hands repeatedly to feel better about this worry, then you would purposely "contaminate" yourself by touching a doorknob without washing your hands.

> **exposure/response prevention (ERP):** practicing "exposure" to the situations that you avoid because of OCD and then not doing your typical response (ritual)

To make this process easier, you will take small steps to get to this point. For example, you may start by touching the doorknob, waiting 3 minutes, and then washing your hands. Then, you will build up tolerance by doing this repeatedly until you get to the point of opening and closing doors entirely without washing your hands! You will do this with all of your avoided or feared situations—so that you will be left with no obsessive rituals. Now, this is the point where you might consider putting this book down or throwing it, begin thinking that this Dr. Zucker is off the wall, or simply stop reading! But DON'T do any of that! You should stay with this book and follow this program for three reasons:

1. You don't want OCD to rule your life anymore and take away the freedom you want and deserve.
2. You will learn many techniques to deal with the anxiety that comes from not doing the rituals, so it won't be *as* hard as you imagine. Plus, you are in charge of your program—YOU will decide the pace and number of steps you want to break it into.

3. Dr. Zucker is not off the wall. She has used this program with hundreds of kids just like you, and all of these children have overcome their OCD! They are no longer ruled by OCD. You are NO different from all of these other kids—you can do it, too!

It is important to understand that your brain will learn from the exposures that these feared and avoided situations are actually not that bad. It is also essential to mention that before we start ERP, you will learn many strategies to manage the anxiety and uncomfortable feelings that come up when you prevent yourself from doing the compulsive behaviors and rituals. It won't always be easy, but you are 100% capable of doing this. This is how you will be a master at challenging OCD. This is how you will win!

Metacognitive Therapy (MCT)

A psychologist named Dr. Adrian Wells, from the United Kingdom, developed a type of cognitive therapy called "metacognitive therapy" (MCT). MCT focuses on your relationship to your thoughts and *how* you think (instead of *what* you think). Metacognition is a basic inner process that is in charge of managing your thinking. Metacognition is responsible for shaping what you focus on and pay attention to. Dr. Wells explained that people with disorders like OCD get their attention stuck on threatening things. He called this problem "cognitive attentional syndrome," which is made up of worry, repetitive thinking patterns, and the tendency to scan the environment for threats.

MCT tries to help people understand their beliefs about their thoughts. For example, you might believe that by thinking about all of the ways that germs can get to you, you are then able to prevent getting contaminated or getting sick. This is a belief that you have formed about your thoughts.

The goal of metacognitive therapy is to change the way you experience and relate to your thoughts and to change how you react to your thoughts or ideas. There are two main MCT techniques that help you switch your attention away from its focus on threat and change the way you experience your thoughts: the attention training technique and the detached mindfulness technique.

1. Attention Training Technique

This technique helps you learn how to switch your focus from one thing to another and how to divide your attention between more than one thing at once. Attention training technique is very effective for the somatic/hyperawareness type of OCD.

For more information on this technique, I recommend that you have your parent(s) or a professional therapist refer to Dr. Wells's book (see the References section in the back of this book) and look at Chapter 4, which gives a script for the technique. You can also visit his website to learn more about ATT. Your parent or therapist can do the recording of the script for you, and you can listen to it twice a day until you are able to master switching your focus and attention away from the OCD-related thoughts. You should listen to the script when you are not anxious or stressed.

2. Detached Mindfulness Technique

This technique teaches you how to be aware (or mindful) of your thoughts and how to become an observer of your thoughts (detachment), rather than a responder to your thoughts. In detached mindfulness, you learn how to recognize that your thought is just a thought. Whether it is true or not, it is only a thought, and nothing else. This will help you to be less reactive to what you are actually thinking about because you will learn how to see the thought as just a thought.

Because this is a different way of thinking about your thoughts, it may sound a little confusing to you. I admit, when I first learned about metacognitive therapy, it took a while for me to really understand the technique and what it had to say about the thoughts part of OCD.

By learning about MCT, you can gain another strategy to use to overcome OCD, as it teaches you how to change your beliefs about your thoughts and how to shift your focus away from OCD-related thoughts. We will go into this technique in more detail in Chapter 5.

Mindfulness

Just as detached mindfulness in MCT teaches you a different way of seeing your thoughts, traditional mindfulness describes a different way of experiencing yourself and the world—almost like a different way of seeing things. During most of your day-to-day life, you are thinking about and focused on what you are doing. Whether it's homework, talking to friends, or watching TV, you likely go through your days busy with thoughts. Having OCD, you also likely worry and get upset about OCD-related thoughts and situations. Worries are thoughts about things that haven't happened yet. In fact, they often are about things that will probably never happen (even though it doesn't feel that way at the time). Worries are about the future, and because they are about the future, they distract you from focusing on what is happening right now in the present moment.

> **mindfulness:** the process of being fully aware of yourself and your thoughts

One goal in dealing with anxiety and OCD is to help you be more focused on being in the present moment, and mindfulness helps you learn how to do this. Like detached mindfulness described previously, mindfulness allows you to gain distance from your thoughts (by identifying them as thoughts and becoming an observer) and simply be in the moment. When you are focused on this exact moment, you will realize that you are okay.

Mindfulness is the process of being fully aware of yourself and your thoughts. When OCD symptoms come up, your focus gets narrow and you are drawn into the obsessions and compulsions. This can be an automatic process. To prevent this from happening, and to make it possible to change the OCD pattern, you want to take a step back and be aware that you are stuck in OCD thinking. You want to refocus on the present moment, rather than staying stuck on an OCD thought.

Mindfulness is a way to get away from your thoughts in a very natural and relaxed way. The deeper part of mindfulness is that it helps you get out of your mind—not in a scary way, or in a way that makes you feel not like yourself, but in an incredibly peaceful way that not only makes you feel like you are okay, but also actually shows you that you are. It helps you be less focused on your thoughts, which leads you to be more focused on the actual experience at hand.

Through practicing mindfulness and learning how to meditate (Chapter 4), you will experience what it feels like to be less attached to your thoughts. This will make it easier to challenge the OCD, as it will be easier to see the OCD as a thought that you can either focus on or not (like in detached mindfulness described previously).

Now that we have reviewed the different approaches to overcoming OCD in detail, let's look at the three parts again, this time with added descriptions of the approaches. Look at the "Body, Thoughts, Behavior" expanded graphic. The arrows point to the methods that you will use to address each part.

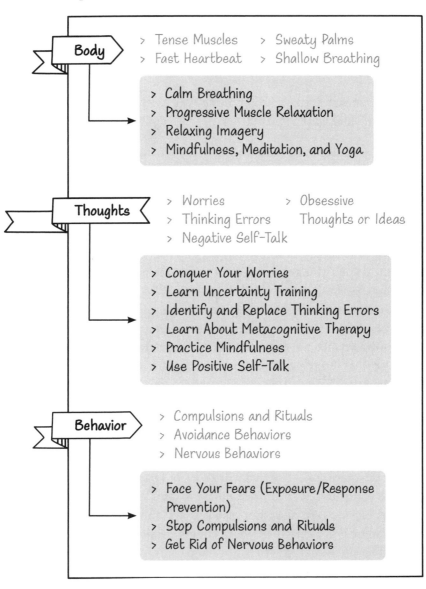

Body
> Tense Muscles   > Sweaty Palms
> Fast Heartbeat   > Shallow Breathing

> Calm Breathing
> Progressive Muscle Relaxation
> Relaxing Imagery
> Mindfulness, Meditation, and Yoga

Thoughts
> Worries   > Obsessive
> Thinking Errors   Thoughts or Ideas
> Negative Self-Talk

> Conquer Your Worries
> Learn Uncertainty Training
> Identify and Replace Thinking Errors
> Learn About Metacognitive Therapy
> Practice Mindfulness
> Use Positive Self-Talk

Behavior
> Compulsions and Rituals
> Avoidance Behaviors
> Nervous Behaviors

> Face Your Fears (Exposure/Response Prevention)
> Stop Compulsions and Rituals
> Get Rid of Nervous Behaviors

Medication

Some children with OCD also benefit from medication, which is usually prescribed by a psychiatrist. You may already be taking medication. Just like there is nothing to feel bad about for having OCD, there is nothing to feel bad about for taking medication to help you treat it. Again, many people with allergies take allergy medications and get better. Similarly, many kids with OCD benefit from medication.

Studies have been done to see which treatment—cognitive-behavioral therapy (CBT), medication, or both combined together—is best for children with OCD. The studies found that the combination of CBT and medication has the best results, but just doing CBT comes very close—that those kids do almost as well, on average, as the kids who have both CBT and medication. Children who *only* take medication, but don't do CBT, don't do nearly as well as either of the other treatment groups. So, although CBT is most important, it may be beneficial to also take medication. However, children should not be on medication without also being in CBT.

The most common type of medication used to treat OCD is called "selective serotonin reuptake inhibitors," or SSRIs. SSRIs work in the brain to prevent the reabsorption of a neurotransmitter called "serotonin," and this ends up making more serotonin available in the brain. For some unknown reason, when there is more serotonin floating around between the neurons, OCD symptoms improve, and people have less OCD thoughts and urges. Common SSRI brand names include Prozac, Zoloft, Luvox, and Paxil. There are also medications that are similar to SSRIs but also work on other neurotransmitters (not just serotonin). These include brand names such as Effexor and Remeron. Another type of medication, Anafranil, is a tricyclic antidepressant that is also very effective for OCD. A doctor will help you decide which medication is the best option.

selective serotonin reuptake inhibitors (SSRIs): medication that works in the brain to prevent the reabsorption of a neurotransmitter called "serotonin," making more of it available in the brain, which helps OCD improve

Anti-anxiety medications, such as Klonopin, Xanax, and Ativan, also are sometimes used to help reduce the feeling of anxiety in children and teens with OCD. They often are given in addition to SSRIs, although they can be given alone. The main caution is that these can cause physical dependence, meaning that if you take these medications for a long period of time, you may feel like you need to keep taking them.

If the SSRIs and anti-anxiety medications are not doing the job and the OCD is really bad, a low dose of mood stabilizers, such as Risperdal, Abilify, Zyprexa, or Seroquel, could be added for additional help.

Studies have shown that a supplement called NAC (N-Acetyl Cysteine), which is an amino acid, is very effective for OCD. Given how safe it is, it's worth trying it. I always recommend checking with your pediatrician or psychiatrist first, as with anything new you might start taking. The dose is 2,400 mg a day (1,200 mg in the morning and 1,200 mg in the evening). From my experience, I have found NAC to be beneficial for OCD and also very effective in reducing motor tics.

Finally, PANDAS/PANS seems to be related to the immune system and inflammation. Therefore, taking supplements such as probiotics and omega-3 fatty acids with more EPA than DHA could help. Antibiotics are also regularly used to treat the strep infections, though it is still unclear if taking these over a long period of time is effective.

To summarize, medication should not be given unless the individual also is receiving help from a therapist skilled in cognitive-behavioral therapy. Also, medication should not be the first choice, as there are side effects. Rather, therapy should be started first, and then if needed, medication should be given for additional benefit. Don't worry, though, if you are already taking medication and haven't been in therapy yet. Reading this book is a great step. Finally, if you are taking medication and experience side effects, make sure to tell your parents and your doctor.

Other Things to Keep in Mind

Being Proactive

To be *proactive* means to take action—to identify a problem and come up with a solution. When you are being proactive, your behavior is a result of your values—of what is important to you, including your larger goals. The opposite is to be *reactive*. When you are being reactive, your behavior is a result of your feelings. Let's use the example of doing your homework. Many times, you won't feel like doing your homework. There are other things you'd rather be doing, like watching TV, playing outside, playing video games, doing your nails, texting, or just doing nothing! If you are being reactive, you won't do your homework because you will decide according to your feelings. You don't feel like it, so you won't do it. However, if you are being proactive, you will do your homework because you will decide according to your values. You don't feel like it, but that doesn't matter because doing your homework and going to school the next day with all of your homework done—and being prepared—is important to you. In other words, it is what you value. Also, once you get started on it, it ends up being fine.

proactive: to take action; to identify a problem and come up with a solution based on your values (rather than your feelings)

You may not always feel like doing the work that's involved with taking control of OCD. At times, it will be hard and you will be challenged. During those times, I encourage you to be *proactive*! Keep reminding yourself that you value working hard to overcome your OCD and that working hard in this program is the way to do it.

Getting Support From Others Who Believe in You

If you were to come into my office and we were to meet in person, one of the first things I would share with you would be that I believe in you and your ability to take control of OCD. I can say this because I've watched hundreds of kids learn these strategies and master them. I know that if you are reading this book, you've got what it takes to do the same. Believing in yourself and having others believe in you is very important to the success of this program. There is no reason why you cannot be 100% successful. If you put 100% in, you will get 100% out. It will start out harder and get easier as you move through it. You will learn what your own process is—what works for you, how you do best, and how you use support from others. You should respect your own process of working through this problem in your life. We want you to be in charge!

Parents, siblings, other family members, and close friends can offer great support, and you should pick at least one or two people who you trust and with whom you feel comfortable talking about this process. Most of the children and teens I have worked with have had to involve their family members—usually their parents—in the treatment process. This is particularly true for family members who have engaged in rituals and compulsions with you. This is very common. Loving, supportive parents end up supporting rituals sometimes because they want you to feel better in a moment of distress. But, as mentioned, the rituals and compulsions only help you in the short term, and overall, they make the OCD worse. If you have parents or others who have helped you do the rituals, or who have made "accommodations" for the OCD, you will need to tell them that they will have to stop. In fact, it can be one of the steps you take in facing your fears and overcoming OCD.

Teach parents and others what you are learning in this book and tell them how they can best support you. Would it be helpful for your mom or dad to tell you that they are proud of you or support you in other ways, like helping you practice the exposures by being there by your side? Could they help by showing affection and hugging you if you have had a tough time with the practices? The goal is to figure out how others can best help you, and to tell them or ask them directly what you want or need from them.

It is your personal choice whether to tell friends and other family members about your OCD. Although most people will be completely understanding and offer their support, some others might be judging or find it difficult to respond in a warm, appropriate way. Regardless of who you choose to tell (or not tell), or what reactions you may get from others, do not forget that OCD is a very common problem, and even more people suffer from anxiety disorders. There is nothing wrong with you for having OCD, and you are working hard and trying your best to take control of OCD!

Be hopeful. Don't doubt or question your strength. This can work, and it will work. Have confidence that you can and will make it work. You will do the things you need to do, step by step, and you will come out on top. You can do it!

What I Know Now

In this chapter, you learned about cognitive-behavioral therapy (CBT) and how OCD has three parts: body, thoughts, and behavior. We reviewed the common body signs, thoughts, and behaviors associated with OCD, and the methods you will learn to treat all three parts. You learned about exposure/response prevention (ERP) and how you will break steps down into smaller steps and go at your own pace. The principles of metacognitive therapy (MCT) and mindfulness were introduced, as they will be helpful, particularly for dealing with the thoughts part of OCD. The option of medication was discussed, and you learned about the common medications used to treat OCD. Finally, you learned about being proactive, being hopeful, and the importance of believing in yourself and having others believe in you.

3

Developing Your Ladder

"Listing all of the things I didn't do because of OCD made it easy to see how much of a problem it was. When we made my ladder, I thought to myself, 'I will never be able to do those steps at the top,' yet when I got to those steps, I was able to do it! All the little steps made it possible to do those at the top, plus I used many strategies that I learned to be able to deal with it."

—Olive, age 11

The purpose of this chapter is to understand the impact of OCD on your life, how it limits what you can do, and how it causes you to do certain things (behaviors you do in response to OCD such as compulsions and rituals). When you are "organized" by something, you are controlled by it, and it influences what you do. It takes away from your freedom to just be and to just focus on what you want to do. When you have OCD, you end up being organized and controlled by it. Now is the time to get a clear understanding of just how much it organizes you and even your family, as well as your behavior. With this understanding, you will begin the goal-setting part of this program.

In this chapter, you will develop your ladder. The ladder will list all of the situations that are hard for you to do because of OCD—situations that you avoid because they cause you anxiety or make you feel uncomfortable. For example, these situations might include using public bathrooms, eating food from sample trays in grocery stores, or not counting the steps when you walk up stairs.

It is important to make the ladder now—early in the book—because it sets the stage for what's to come. You will use the ladder during the exposure phase beginning in Chapter 9. Even though you will learn a lot of coping strategies and techniques before it comes time to do the steps on the ladder, doing it now is an essential step in this program. It lays out the goals in the beginning of the process, and this will make it flow better later on.

Making Your Ladder

At the end of this chapter, there is a page that has a drawing of a ladder. You can choose to actually use this one and write in the book, or you can make your own ladder on a separate sheet of paper or a larger poster board. It's important that you make an actual ladder and not just consider it in your mind or even just write it out as a list. In my work with children, I cut a poster board in half and use good-smelling Mr. Sketch markers to make the ladder. You should try to make your ladder visually clear—so that when you look at it, it's easy to read and see what steps are included.

The first step in making your ladder is to list all of the situations that you avoid because of OCD on a separate sheet of paper. You want to write the list in a positive way, describing what you *should* or *would* be doing if you didn't have OCD. For example, if you don't touch doorknobs with your hands, you would write it as "touch doorknobs with hands." If you do four checking ritual behaviors before you leave the house every morning, you would write it as "leave house without checking oven, toaster, back door, and Sniffy and Cassidy (the dogs)."

ladder: *a list of all of the situations that are hard for you to do because of OCD; situations that you avoid because they cause you anxiety or make you feel uncomfortable*

If it is hard to start writing things out this way, you can first list all of the rituals and OCD behaviors that you do and all of the things you avoid. Then, you can change them over, or convert them, to describe what you should be doing, or what you would like to be able to do—like touch doorknobs with your hands.

The list should be very thorough, and you may ask your family members for ideas of what to include, as they are probably aware of your OCD behaviors. Include all rituals that you do to make the obsessive thoughts, ideas, or images better. List every behavior that is done in response to the OCD thoughts.

Once you have listed all of the behaviors and rituals, and the situations that you avoid, then you want to put them in order, numbering them from easiest to hardest. Some kids like to use note cards to write out each situation and then lay them all out on the floor and put them in order this way—laying out the easier ones on the bottom and then the harder ones on the top. You can do this, or just number the items (for example, from 1 to 15, with 1 being the easiest and 15 being the hardest) on the sheet of paper. Every person has a different number of steps on their ladder. There is no set number, but I do recommend having at least 8–10 steps. Many people have up to 40 items, which becomes a two-sided ladder. Don't worry about the length; just focus more on being thorough. Also, you can break steps down into smaller steps. Using the example above, you can break down "leave house without checking oven, toaster, back door, and Sniffy and Cassidy" into four steps: "leave house without checking oven," "leave house without checking oven and toaster," "leave house without checking oven, toaster, and back door," and "leave house without checking oven, toaster, back door, and Sniffy and Cassidy." You are in charge of deciding how many smaller steps you will break the steps down into, and this may be something that you won't decide upon until you are actually in the exposure phase (when you practice the steps).

This brings up another point: Once you are doing the exposures, you may find that you want to make changes to your ladder—either by adding steps, changing the order, breaking them down further into smaller steps, or getting rid of steps that no longer fit. This may happen as your understanding of your OCD improves. This is perfectly fine, and for this reason, it is best to leave some space in between steps on the ladder or even leave a few steps blank.

To help you understand how ladders work, and maybe even get some ideas on what to include in your own ladder, let's go through the examples from Chapter 1 to show how other kids and teens made their ladders.

EXAMPLE 1
Andrew, 12 years old, OCD: Contamination Type

Event: Use public bathroom.

Thought: I can't touch the toilet, flusher, faucets, or doorknob because there are dangerous germs on all of them. Maybe I touched someone's germs and will get sick.

Feeling: Very, very anxious!

Action: Wash hands and use paper towels to turn off faucet and open doorknob.

Andrew worried constantly about getting contaminated with germs and getting sick. He avoided any surface that he thought might have germs on it, and also avoided people who he thought might get him sick. Andrew tried his best to avoid public bathrooms, but he ended up having to use them in school. When he did use public bathrooms, he would do his best to avoid touching the lock on the door, the flusher, the sink, and the doorknob. He used paper towels and toilet paper to navigate his way through the bathroom.

List of Avoided Situations and OCD–Related Behaviors

> Use public bathrooms
> Use public bathroom and wash hands for 15 seconds

> Use bathroom and wash hands for 5 seconds
> Use bathroom and wash hands without reciting alphabet in head
> Touch lock on bathroom door with hands (not sleeve)
> Touch toilet with hands (not toilet paper)
> Touch flusher with hands
> Touch faucet
> Use first paper towel from dispenser
> Touch doorknob or handle with hands
> Sit next to someone for one minute after they sneezed
> Walk by the pharmacy part of the drugstore
> Have lunch near a sick kid
> Go to a friend's house after the friend was sick last week
> Touch doorknobs and handles in public places
> Go to a friend's house without asking about recent illnesses

Once Andrew listed his items, he ranked them in order (with 1 being the easiest and 16 being the hardest):

5	Use public bathrooms
13	Use public bathroom and wash hands for 15 seconds
10	Use bathroom and wash hands for 5 seconds
9	Use bathroom and wash hands without reciting alphabet in head
12	Touch lock on bathroom door with hands (not sleeve)
16	Touch toilet with hands (not toilet paper)
14	Touch flusher with hands
8	Touch faucet
6	Use first paper towel from dispenser
11	Touch doorknob or handle of bathroom with hands
3	Sit next to someone for one minute after he or she sneezed
1	Walk by the pharmacy part of the drugstore

15	Have lunch near a sick kid
4	Go to a friend's house after the friend was sick last week
7	Touch doorknobs and handles in public places
2	Go to a friend's house without asking about recent illnesses

After ranking them in order from easiest to hardest, Andrew wrote in all of the steps on his ladder, with the easiest at the bottom and the hardest at the top:

Touch toilet with hands (not toilet paper)

Have lunch near a sick kid

Touch flusher with hands

Use public bathroom and wash hands for 15 seconds

Touch lock on bathroom door with hands

Touch doorknob or handle of bathroom with hands

Use bathroom and wash hands for 5 seconds

Use bathroom and wash hands without reciting alphabet in head

Touch faucet

Touch doorknobs and handles in public places

Use first paper towel from dispenser

Use public bathrooms

Go to a friend's house after the friend was sick last week

Sit next to someone for one minute after they sneezed

Go to a friend's house without asking about recent illnesses

Walk by the pharmacy part of the drugstore

EXAMPLE 2

Alicia, 11 years old, OCD: Contamination Type

Event: Eat cookie from bake sale.

Thought: What if the person who baked it was sick? Now I will get their germs and be sick, too! The eggs could have salmonella in them, or the ingredients could be old and expired! What if I throw up?

Feeling: Very, very anxious!

Action: Ask Mom for reassurance that the cookies were safe. Ask friends if they ate cookies from the bake sale and see how they are feeling. Wait 3 days until I feel sure that I didn't get sick from bake sale cookies.

Like Andrew, Alicia worried constantly about getting contaminated with germs and getting sick. However, her worries centered on getting sick from eating food, particularly spoiled food. She avoided eating food from outside of her home as much as possible, but when she did, she would worry that she would get sick and ask her mom to reassure her that she was okay. She avoided foods that she labeled as "dangerous" because they were foods that people got sick from (they either had been recalled or had been causes of illness in the past, like mad cow disease). Other foods, like grilled cheese and pizza, also made her anxious, although she didn't really know why. They just seemed like foods that might make her sick.

List of Avoided Situations and OCD-Related Behaviors

> Eat grilled cheese and pizza
> Eat meat at home without asking questions about it
> Eat meat from a BBQ at a friend's house
> Eat meat that has been left out on the counter for 2 hours
> Eat food from a bake sale
> Eat sample food in a grocery store
> Make cookies and eat some raw cookie dough
> Eat yogurt and drink milk without checking the expiration date
> Eat expired chips
> Drink milk that expired 1 day ago, then 2 days ago

> Don't ask Mom for reassurance
> Eat tomatoes and spinach
> Sit next to someone who was recently sick
> Watch videos of people throwing up and imagine throwing up
> Eat unwashed grapes

Once Alicia listed her items, she ranked them in order (with 1 being the easiest and 15 being the hardest):

4	Eat grilled cheese and pizza
3	Eat meat at home without asking questions about it
7	Eat meat from a BBQ at a friend's house
14	Eat meat that has been left out on the counter for 2 hours
2	Eat food from a bake sale
1	Eat sample food in a grocery store
15	Make cookies and eat some raw cookie dough
6	Eat yogurt and drink milk without checking the expiration date
12	Eat expired chips
13	Drink milk that expired 1 day ago, then 2 days ago
9	Don't ask Mom for reassurance
5	Eat tomatoes and spinach
10	Sit next to someone who was recently sick
11	Watch videos of people throwing up and imagine throwing up
8	Eat unwashed grapes

After ranking them in order from easiest to hardest, Alicia wrote in all of the steps on her ladder:

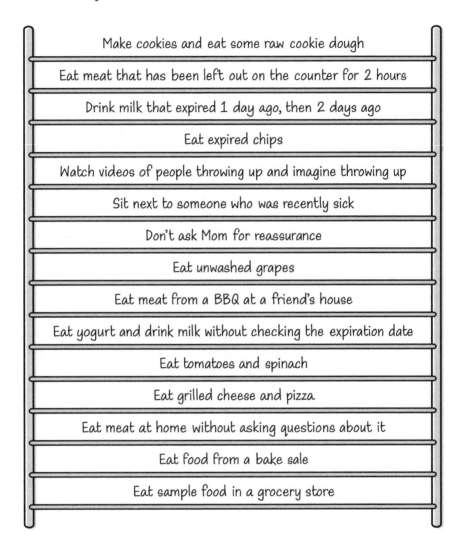

Make cookies and eat some raw cookie dough

Eat meat that has been left out on the counter for 2 hours

Drink milk that expired 1 day ago, then 2 days ago

Eat expired chips

Watch videos of people throwing up and imagine throwing up

Sit next to someone who was recently sick

Don't ask Mom for reassurance

Eat unwashed grapes

Eat meat from a BBQ at a friend's house

Eat yogurt and drink milk without checking the expiration date

Eat tomatoes and spinach

Eat grilled cheese and pizza

Eat meat at home without asking questions about it

Eat food from a bake sale

Eat sample food in a grocery store

EXAMPLE 3

Tyler, 13 years old, OCD: Emotional Contamination Type

Event: Think about high school boy who committed suicide.

Thought: Why would he have killed himself? What was he thinking? What were his thoughts that made him commit suicide? What if I think about the thoughts he could have had and then I mistake them for my own thoughts and commit suicide also? What if no one knew that I didn't really mean to kill myself?

Feeling: Very, very anxious and scared!

Action: Ask for reassurance, "I'm not suicidal, right?" from parents. Avoid listening to a song that triggers those thoughts.

Tyler's OCD caused him great distress. He experienced his thoughts as very powerful and all-consuming, and even though the thoughts were symptoms of OCD, he felt they were real. This caused him to feel unstable, like he couldn't trust his thoughts. It all started when he heard about a 16-year-old boy who committed suicide. It was so upsetting to him, and he couldn't imagine ever feeling so badly that he would kill himself. As he started to feel confused about what this boy could possibly have been thinking at the time he committed suicide, Tyler began to imagine what the boy could have thought. Although he never came up with any specific thoughts that he imagined the boy had, Tyler had the disturbing worry that by imagining the thoughts, he would have those thoughts in his head and mistake them for own. Then he worried that if he had those imagined thoughts, he would commit suicide just as the high school boy had. He further worried that if he did kill himself, his loved ones wouldn't have known that he wasn't actually suicidal and that it was only because he had been thinking the thoughts of the other boy.

In health class, they talked about suicide and this was very triggering for him. Then, a song came out by Logic ("1-800-273-8255") on suicide prevention, and the lyrics "I just want to die . . . I don't want to be alive" triggered Tyler and he avoided the song. He also asked his parents (and me) for reassurance that he was not suicidal. In addition to these thoughts, he had other symptoms around thoughts almost being contagious. If someone gave their opinion on something, he would start to blur their opinion with his own and worry that he would "catch" their opinion and it would become his own. Tyler also began to worry about being near certain other kids because he thought that, if he spent too much time with them, they could steal his smarts and he would no longer be smart. He also avoided other kids with physical or intellectual disabilities, fearing that by being near them, he would become disabled. Tyler also was afraid to bring the garbage cans into the garage, fearing that if he did so, he might become a waste collector. He felt guilty and stressed about his thoughts. Tyler said, "I feel like I'm in my head all the time, and it's making it hard to know what is really happening sometimes." He had self-doubt and felt that he couldn't fully trust himself.

List of Avoided Situations and OCD-Related Behaviors

> Listen to song by Logic
> Read accounts of people who have attempted (and survived) suicide
> Read a book on a teen who was depressed (such as *All the Bright Places*)
> Have thoughts about high school boy's suicide without seeking reassurance
> Randomly comment, "Ugh, I'm going to kill myself!"
> Bring the garbage in to garage twice a week
> Say hello to the waste collectors
> Drive through the waste and recycling center; wave to the employees
> Have lunch with the kids who may steal my smarts
> Volunteer with children who have intellectual disabilities
> Watch videos on children who have lost a limb
> Talk to an amputee
> Ask friends to share their opinions
> Confidently share my opinions when they differ from others'

Once Tyler listed his items, he ranked them in order (with 1 being the easiest and 14 being the hardest):

12	Listen to song by Logic
13	Read accounts of people who have attempted (and survived) suicide
7	Read a book on a teen who was depressed (such as *All the Bright Places*)

14	Have thoughts about high school boy's suicide without seeking reassurance
8	Randomly comment, "Ugh, I'm going to kill myself!"
3	Bring the garbage in to garage twice a week
1	Say hello to the waste collectors
2	Drive through the waste and recycling center; wave to the employees
5	Have lunch with the kids who may steal your smarts
10	Volunteer with children who have intellectual disabilities
9	Watch videos on children who have lost a limb
11	Talk to an amputee
4	Ask friends to share their opinions
6	Confidently share your opinions when they differ from others'

After ranking them in order from easiest to hardest, Tyler wrote in all of the steps on his ladder:

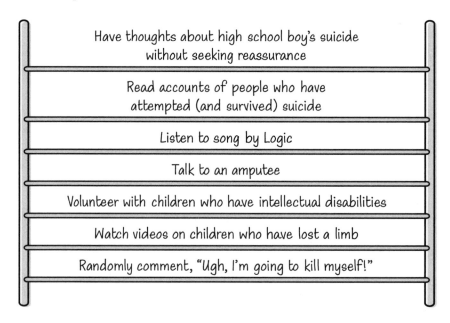

Read a book on a teen who was depressed
(such as *All the Bright Places*)

Confidently share my opinions when they differ from others

Have lunch with the kids who may steal my smarts

Ask friends to share their opinions

Bring the garbage in to garage twice a week

Drive through the waste and recycling
center; wave to the employees

Say hello to the waste collectors

EXAMPLE 4
Sydney, 10 years old, OCD: Doubting/Indecisiveness Types

Event: Step on something.

Thought: What if I stepped on a bug and killed it?

Feeling: Very, very anxious!

Action: Go back and check sidewalk.

Sydney's OCD caused her to doubt and question many things, including her own actions. She would do something and then feel unsure if she had done it or not. To get rid of this uncomfortable feeling, she would tell her mom the details of her actions and let her mom be the judge of whether Sydney had done it or not. Sydney also struggled to make decisions and would often get stuck on a meaningless decision for hours. For example, she would stand in front of the kitchen pantry for 40 minutes, unable to decide on which snack to eat.

List of Avoided Situations and OCD-Related Behaviors

> Step on pencil on purpose and don't report to Mom
> Decide on a snack in 20 minutes, then 10 minutes, then less than 5 minutes

> Use the bathroom and step on toilet paper on purpose
> Don't tell or confess to Mom 2 days this week, then 3, 5, and 7 days
> Decide on what to wear in 5–10 minutes
> Decide on what to have for dinner in 2 minutes or less
> Decide on whom to make plans with in 5 minutes or less
> Decide on whom to sit with at assembly in 3 seconds
> State what I did during the day without doubting if it happened
> Don't check to see if I stepped on something
> Walk through the woods and step on sticks and don't report to Mom
> Light a candle and then blow it out without telling Mom

Once Sydney listed her items, she ranked them in order (with 1 being the easiest and 12 being the hardest):

4	Step on pencil on purpose and don't report to Mom
7	Decide on a snack in 20 minutes, then 10 minutes, then less than 5 minutes
1	Use the bathroom and step on toilet paper on purpose
8	Don't tell or confess to Mom 2 days this week, then 3, 5, 7 days
2	Decide on what to wear in 5–10 minutes
9	Decide on what to have for dinner in 2 minutes or less
6	Decide on whom to make plans with in 5 minutes or less
3	Decide on whom to sit with at assembly in 3 seconds
11	State what I did during the day without doubting if it happened
5	Don't check to see if I stepped on something
12	Walk through the woods and step on sticks and don't report to Mom
10	Light a candle and then blow it out without telling Mom

After ranking them in order from easiest to hardest, Sydney wrote in all of the steps on her ladder:

Walk through the woods and step on sticks and don't report to Mom

State what I did during the day without doubting if it happened

Light a candle and then blow it out without telling Mom

Decide on what to have for dinner in 2 minutes or less

Don't tell or confess to Mom 2 days this week, then 3, 5, and 7 days

Decide on a snack in 20 minutes, then 10 minutes, then less than 5 minutes

Decide on whom to make plans with in 5 minutes or less

Don't check to see if I stepped on something

Step on pencil on purpose and don't report to Mom

Decide on whom to sit with at assembly in 3 seconds

Decide on what to wear in 5–10 minutes

Use the bathroom and step on toilet paper on purpose

> **EXAMPLE 5**
> Connor, 16 years old, OCD: Harm Type
> _____
>
> **Event:** Someone sneezes near you at school.
>
> **Thought:** What if I am sick and I spread germs and get someone else sick? What if I have the flu? What if I spread it and someone dies?
>
> **Feeling:** Very, very anxious!
>
> **Action:** Keep distance from others, avoid lunchroom and eat alone in classroom instead, and use shirt to open doors. Avoid social plans for a few days to ensure I'm not really sick and don't have the flu.

Connor's OCD focused on causing harm to others, and he worried that he could do something that could have a bad outcome for others. For example, in addition to worrying about getting others sick, he took a lot of precautions at home. Before leaving the house, he would check that the oven and stove were off and that his mother's hair dryer was unplugged, and before going to bed at night, he checked to make sure all of the doors and windows were locked. He also regularly charged his mother's phone because he worried that she would go out and run out of battery and that if she got a flat tire or needed assistance, her phone wouldn't have enough charge. Connor also worried about stepping on animals or running over them when he drove. He regularly drove on a route again to look for dead animals and would retrace his steps when walking in the neighborhood. Connor's OCD impacted him socially, as he was anxious most of the time he was with friends because he was worried that he would do something by accident that could hurt them, such as make a plan to go to the movies. He would worry that they could get in an accident on the way there and that he would be responsible.

List of Avoided Situations and OCD-Related Behaviors

> Mom leaves the house with 50% battery on phone
> Do not check Mom's phone
> Someone sneezes near me and I continue on as usual
> Initiate a plan with friends to go to one place
> Initiate a plan with friends to go to three places
> Go to bed without checking doors

> Go to bed without checking doors and windows
> Leave the house without checking Mom's hair dryer
> Leave the house without checking the stove and oven
> Leave the house without checking anything
> Do not drive back to check for animals
> Drive over a bumpy road without checking for animals
> Walk around the neighborhood without retracing steps

Once Connor listed his items, he ranked them in order (with 1 being the easiest and 13 being the hardest):

10	Mom leaves the house with 50% battery on phone
11	Do not check Mom's phone
9	Someone sneezes near me and I continue on as usual
7	Initiate a plan with friends to go to one place
8	Initiate a plan with friends to go to three places
1	Go to bed without checking doors
2	Go to bed without checking doors and windows
5	Leave the house without checking Mom's hair dryer
4	Leave the house without checking the stove and oven
6	Leave the house without checking anything
12	Do not drive back to check for animals
13	Drive over a bumpy road without checking for animals
3	Walk around the neighborhood without retracing steps

After ranking them in order from easiest to hardest, Connor wrote in all of the steps on his ladder:

Drive over a bumpy road without checking for animals
Do not drive back to check for animals
Do not check Mom's phone
Mom leaves the house with 50% battery on phone
Someone sneezes near me and I continue on as usual
Initiate a plan with friends to go to three places
Initiate a plan with friends to go to one place
Leave the house without checking anything
Leave the house without checking Mom's hair dryer
Leave the house without checking the stove and oven
Walk around the neighborhood without retracing steps
Go to bed without checking doors and windows
Go to bed without checking doors

EXAMPLE 6
William, 16 years old, OCD: Scrupulosity Type

Event: Asked to go to a party with friends.

Thought: I shouldn't have fun or else I will be punished. Something bad will happen if I enjoy myself and feel pleasure.

Feeling: Very, very anxious!

Action: Tell my friends that I can't go. Stay home and do homework instead.

William's OCD led him to feel a strong sense of guilt any time he did something he enjoyed or labeled unnecessary, and the more enjoyable or unnecessary the activity, the guiltier he felt. His OCD held him back from doing things that all of his other friends were able to do, like go out on the weekends and enjoy himself, play video games for hours, and pursue dating girls. He really liked girls, especially one in particular, but could never ask any out because he feared that the guilt would be too strong. In fact, he had never held hands with a girl and certainly never kissed one. Although he had perfect attendance at school and A's in every class, he was not enjoying the feeling of success because his social life was lacking so much. William could not identify a true reason why he felt this way, and he acknowledged that it didn't make sense and was irrational. But the feeling was so strong that it ruled his life.

List of Avoided Situations and OCD-Related Behaviors

> Go to a party on the weekend
> Make a plan for all of my friends to go out on a weekend
> Go to the movies on a weeknight
> Don't do homework on weekend nights (except during exam week)
> Talk to a girl for an extended period of time
> Ask a girl for her number
> Hold hands with a girl
> Kiss a girl
> Play video games for 2 hours
> Invite friends over on a weeknight
> Skip school one day and go to the movies (with parents' permission!)
> Think about girls I like, even if I start feeling guilty when doing so
> Eat three desserts in one night
> Go on vacation and miss 2 days of school

Once William listed his items, he ranked them in order (with 1 being the easiest and 14 being the hardest):

4	Go to a party on the weekend
6	Make a plan for all of my friends to go out on a weekend
9	Go to the movies on a weeknight

1	Don't do homework on weekend nights (except during exam week)
7	Talk to a girl for an extended period of time
12	Ask a girl for her number
13	Hold hands with a girl
14	Kiss a girl
2	Play video games for 2 hours
3	Invite friends over on a weeknight
10	Skip school one day and go to the movies (with parents' permission!)
5	Think about girls I like, even if I start feeling guilty when doing so
8	Eat three desserts in one night
11	Go on vacation with family or friends and miss 2 days of school

After ranking them in order from easiest to hardest, William wrote in all of the steps on his ladder:

Kiss a girl
Hold hands with a girl
Ask a girl for her number
Go on vacation with family or friends and miss 2 days of school
Skip school one day and go to the movies (with parents' permission!)
Go to the movies on a weeknight
Eat three desserts in one night
Talk to a girl for an extended period of time
Make a plan for all of my friends to go out on a weekend

Think about girls I like, even if I start feeling guilty when doing so

Go to a party on the weekend

Invite friends over on a weeknight

Play video games for 2 hours

Don't do homework on weekend nights (except during exam week)

Note that William's ladder includes steps that may seem a bit irresponsible (missing school, eating three desserts in one night), but his steps were designed to address his difficulties with feeling pleasure and enjoyment. This ladder is not a typical example, and William's parents were very supportive of each step on his ladder and knew that it was important for him to do things that he considered "wrong" to challenge his scrupulosity-type OCD.

EXAMPLE 7
Jasmine, 15 years old, OCD: Symmetry/"Just Feels Right" Types

Event: Look at desk.

Thought: Things are out of order. They need to be straight.

Feeling: Very, very uncomfortable!

Action: Order and arrange everything until it is all lined up.

Jasmine struggled to feel comfortable unless things were in order and felt right around her. She spent a good amount of time every day straightening her desk and arranging things in her room until it felt right to her. She couldn't stand having the closet door cracked open, things needed to be perfectly aligned on her desk, with everything facing the right way, and when she slept at night, her covers needed to lie evenly over her. If any of these conditions were not met, Jasmine would feel physically uncomfortable and couldn't relax. When Jasmine walked into a room, she noticed the angles and randomly saw connecting lines, and she couldn't help but focus on making the lines seem straight by connecting them as perfect squares.

List of Avoided Situations and OCD-Related Behaviors

> Have one or two things that are not perfectly aligned on the desk and leave them there
> Have a "messy" desk without fixing it
> Sleep over at a friend's house where everything is out of order and "messy"
> Leave paper partially sticking out of a folder
> Mismatch shoes in closet
> Wear two different black socks to school
> Walk into room and change straight, square lines to squiggly, crooked ones and draw it
> Let brother come in room and move things around without telling me
> Stare at a backward-written letter on a piece of paper (such as a backward "R")
> Let Dad come in room and put books out of order
> Leave backpack zipper partially opened
> Sleep with closet door cracked open a bit
> Leave closet door open halfway for a whole day
> Leave broken pen cap on pen and sticking out of pen holder
> Turn two, then four, then eight things around in room
> Turn clock upside down on wall and leave it there for one week
> Sleep with blanket laid unevenly upon me
> Pack an odd number of underwear, shorts, and T-shirts for camp this summer

Once Jasmine listed her items, she ranked them in order (with 1 being the easiest and 18 being the hardest):

9	Have 1–2 things that are not perfectly aligned on the desk and leave them there
5	Have a "messy" desk without fixing it
2	Sleep over at a friend's house where everything is out of order and "messy"

4	Leave paper partially sticking out of folder
7	Mismatch shoes in closet
13	Wear two different black socks to school
10	Walk into room and change straight, square lines to squiggly, crooked ones and draw it
16	Let brother come in room and move things around without telling me
8	Stare at a backward-written letter on a piece of paper (such as a backward "R")
15 .	Let Dad come in room and put books out of order
1	Leave backpack zipper partially opened
11	Sleep with closet door cracked open a bit
12	Leave closet door open halfway for a whole day
6	Leave broken pen cap on pen and sticking out of pen holder
14	Turn two, then four, then eight things around in room
18	Turn clock upside down on wall and leave it there for one week
17	Sleep with blanket laid unevenly upon me
3	Pack an odd number of underwear, shorts, and T-shirts for camp this summer

After ranking them in order from easiest to hardest, Jasmine wrote in all of the steps on her ladder:

Turn clock upside down on wall and leave it there for one week

Sleep with blanket laid unevenly upon me

Let brother come in room and move things around without telling me

Let Dad come in room and put books out of order

Turn two, then four, then eight things around in room

Wear two different black socks to school

Leave closet door open halfway for a whole day

Sleep with closet door cracked open a bit

Walk into room and change straight, square lines to squiggly, crooked ones and draw it

Have one or two things that are not perfectly aligned on desk and leave them there

Stare at a backward-written letter on a piece of paper (such as a backward "R")

Mismatch shoes in closet

Leave broken pen cap on pen and sticking out of pen holder

Have a "messy" desk without fixing it

Leave paper partially sticking out of folder

Pack an odd number of underwear, shorts, and T-shirts for camp this summer

Sleep over at a friend's house where everything is out of order and "messy"

Leave backpack zipper partially opened

EXAMPLE 8

Lina, 12 years old, OCD: Sexual Orientation Type

Event: Changing in girls' locker room for PE. A friend is talking to me while we are changing, so I look in her direction.

Thought: What if I'm really looking at her because I want to see her without a shirt? What if she sees me looking at her? What if I have feelings for her? What if I'm a lesbian?

Feeling: Very, very anxious!

Action: Keep the conversation short, look away, avoid talking to my friend for the rest of PE. Scan body for signs of attraction.

Lina's OCD came up at the age of 11, which is often when romantic feelings begin for girls. I met her at 12. Around age 11 to 12, many tweens begin to have crushes. Although she had nothing against how others self-identified, and in fact, knew and admired a few of her older sister's friends who identified as straight, gay, or bisexual, she was worried that she was a lesbian. Lina wasn't attracted to other girls, but she second guessed this and thought she couldn't really know for sure. When her best friend came over for a sleepover and changed in front of her, Lina became embarrassed and uncomfortable. The same thing happened at PE class and at a pool party over the summer. She looked at her friends as they undressed, trying to see if she had romantic feelings or physical attraction. This was actually a compulsion, as she was checking to see if her obsessive thought about being a lesbian was real or not. Because this was making her anxious, she started to avoid sleepovers and sleepover parties. She even missed a few days of PE because she was so stressed out about being in the locker room. A girl in her class came out as lesbian, and Lina avoided her because she was afraid that she would make a move to kiss her and Lina wouldn't know what to do. She thought that if she kissed her back, she would realize that she was a lesbian. Around this time, a boy gave her a note that he liked her, and she thought she might like him but felt it was unfair to tell him that in case she was a lesbian. She read about girls who came out as lesbian to see if she could identify with their stories and how they discovered that they were lesbian. Lina also asked her parents what would happen if she was lesbian, and they were very reassuring and explained that there was nothing wrong with that and that they would love her no matter what.

List of Avoided Situations and OCD-Related Behaviors

> Write a note back to the boy and tell him I like him also
> Invite best friend over for a sleepover
> Go to a sleepover party
> Change for PE in the locker room and be the last to leave
> While I'm changing into PE clothes, start a conversation with others
> While I'm changing into PE clothes, give someone a compliment on how in shape they are
> Hang out with girl who came out as lesbian; make a plan for after school
> Read a romantic teen novel about heterosexual love

Once Lina listed her items, she ranked them in order (with 1 being the easiest and 8 being the hardest):

6	Write a note back to the boy and tell him I like him also
2	Invite best friend for a sleepover
3	Go to a sleepover party
4	Change for PE in the locker room and be the last to leave
5	While I'm changing into PE clothes, start a conversation with others
8	While I'm changing into PE clothes, give someone a compliment on how in shape they are
7	Hang out with girl who came out as lesbian; make a plan for after school
1	Read a romantic teen novel about heterosexual love

After ranking them in order from easiest to hardest, Lina wrote in all of the steps on her ladder:

While I'm changing into PE clothes, give someone
a compliment on how in shape they are

Hang out with girl who came out as lesbian;
make a plan for after school

Write a note back to the boy and tell him I like him also

While I'm changing into PE clothes, start a conversation with others

Change for PE in the locker room and be the last to leave

Go to a sleepover party

Invite best friend for a sleepover

Read a romantic teen novel about heterosexual love

EXAMPLE 9
Kevin, 14 years old, OCD: Pedophilia Type

Event: Walk by a park with other kids playing.

Thought: What if I hurt one of those kids or touched their privates? What if someone knew my thoughts? Does thinking it mean that I did it? Is it as bad as doing it?

Feeling: Very, very anxious!

Action: Shake head four times to the right, quickly and forcefully.

Like William, Kevin worried about doing something bad, even though there was no reason for him to feel like he had done anything wrong (because he hadn't). Kevin's worries were different, though, and had a different theme. Kevin worried about hurting other children, particularly younger ones, and about touching them inappropriately. He never came close to doing this behavior and didn't actually feel sexual feelings toward younger children, but he wor-

ried that he would feel sexual or have sensations in his body. These thoughts were unwanted, intrusive, and caused Kevin to doubt who he was. He also worried about going to jail and being rejected by everyone he knows. Kevin was extremely distressed about these thoughts and also very embarrassed that he had them at all.

An Important Note: With this type of OCD, I reassure clients in the beginning of treatment that they are not pedophiles. The thoughts are experienced as unwanted and distressing and what is called "ego-dystonic," meaning that they don't, or sync, with their understanding of themselves. The opposite is "ego-syntonic," which is when the thoughts are consistent with who you are and feel like a fit. With actual pedophiles, the thoughts are ego-syntonic, and they don't see their actions as a problem.

List of Avoided Situations and OCD–Related Behaviors

> Walk by a park
> Walk by a school playground
> Talk to younger children
> Play with younger children
> Babysit younger cousins
> Read about sexual predators
> Have thoughts without shaking head at all
> Read *My Body Is Private* or similar book for children about private parts
> Talk to parents about thoughts
> Think about lighting a candle and then light one (to show the difference between thought and action)
> Think about winning a million dollars (to show the difference between thought and action)

Once Kevin listed his items, he ranked them in order (with 1 being the easiest and 11 being the hardest):

5	Walk by a park
6	Walk by a school playground
8	Talk to younger children

9	Play with younger children
11	Babysit younger cousins
7	Read about sexual predators
10	Have thoughts without shaking head at all
3	Read *My Body Is Private* or similar book for children about private parts
4	Talk to parents about thoughts
2	Think about lighting a candle and then light one
1	Think about winning a million dollars

After ranking them in order from easiest to hardest, Kevin wrote in all of the steps on his ladder:

Babysit younger cousins

Have thoughts without shaking head at all

Play with younger children

Talk to younger children

Read about sexual predators

Walk by a school playground

Walk by a park

Talk to parents about thoughts

Read *My Body Is Private* or similar book for children about private parts

Think about lighting a candle and then light one

Think about winning a million dollars

> **EXAMPLE 10**
> Talia, 17 years old, OCD: Hypochondria/Health Type
>
> ---
>
> **Event:** Heard about a girl who was diagnosed with leukemia.
>
> **Thought:** What if I have leukemia? What if I die from it? What if the treatments don't work for me?
>
> **Feeling:** Very, very anxious!
>
> **Action:** Ask Mom for reassurance that she isn't sick. Request to see a doctor for bloodwork. Read about symptoms of leukemia in teens online. Read stories about teens who've been diagnosed with leukemia. Scan body for signs of illness.

Talia's OCD caused her to be preoccupied with health and getting sick. She overreacted to colds, worrying that she might die. She scanned her body for symptoms and worried about getting a terminal disease. When she heard about someone who was sick, she would start to feel badly and worried that she would also get sick. She would also ask them questions, such as "How did you know you were sick? What symptoms did you have at first?" She would Google symptoms and ask her parents to bring her to a doctor. When she came in to see me, she would show me marks on her skin and ask if I thought they might be cancerous. She also had some superstitious behaviors and wouldn't wear certain clothes or shoes if she was feeling sick.

List of Avoided Situations and OCD-Related Behaviors

> Hear about someone who is sick and don't ask any questions
> Read about teens with leukemia and other serious conditions
> See a mark on my skin and don't seek reassurance
> Be around someone who was sick and say "I'm sorry you were sick" without asking any questions
> Only go to the doctor for annual visits and if parents suggest it
> Have a symptom and do not Google it
> Wait a week after having a symptom before asking parents for reassurance
> Ask Mom for reassurance and she doesn't give it to me

> Watch a video on a girl my age with leukemia; differentiate from her
> Feel sick and wear clothes and shoes I usually avoid wearing

Once Talia listed her items, she ranked them in order (with 1 being the easiest and 10 being the hardest):

3	Hear about someone who is sick and don't ask any questions
7	Read about teens with leukemia and other serious conditions
5	See a mark on my skin and don't seek reassurance
1	Be around someone who was sick and say "I'm sorry you were sick" without asking any questions
6	Only go to the doctor for annual visits and if parents suggest it
8	Have a symptom and do not Google it
7	Wait a week after having a symptom before asking parents for reassurance
2	Ask Mom for reassurance and she doesn't give it to me
10	Watch a video on a girl my age with leukemia; differentiate from her
4	Feel sick and wear clothes and shoes I usually avoid wearing

After ranking them in order from easiest to hardest, Talia wrote in all of the steps on her ladder:

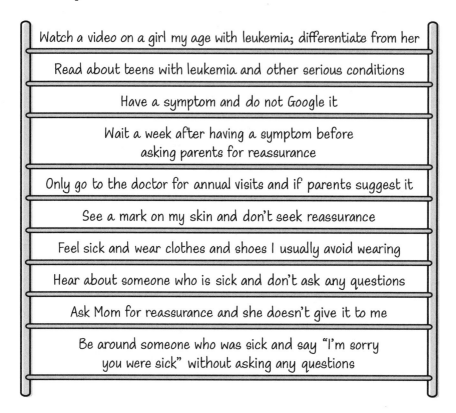

Watch a video on a girl my age with leukemia; differentiate from her

Read about teens with leukemia and other serious conditions

Have a symptom and do not Google it

Wait a week after having a symptom before asking parents for reassurance

Only go to the doctor for annual visits and if parents suggest it

See a mark on my skin and don't seek reassurance

Feel sick and wear clothes and shoes I usually avoid wearing

Hear about someone who is sick and don't ask any questions

Ask Mom for reassurance and she doesn't give it to me

Be around someone who was sick and say "I'm sorry you were sick" without asking any questions

Hopefully, by reviewing the 10 examples and seeing the process of creating the ladders, you are starting to have some ideas about what you want to include in your own ladder and are inspired to make it. Again, it is very important to go ahead and make your ladder now. Good luck!

What I Know Now

This chapter focused on explaining the process of making your ladder, which is the goal-setting part of the program. We reviewed the 10 cases of OCD introduced in Chapter 1, and you saw how each of their ladders were developed.

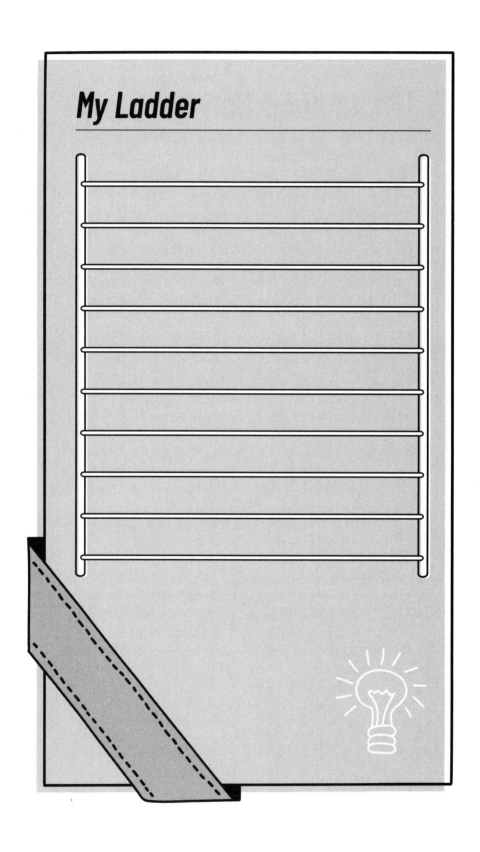

My Ladder

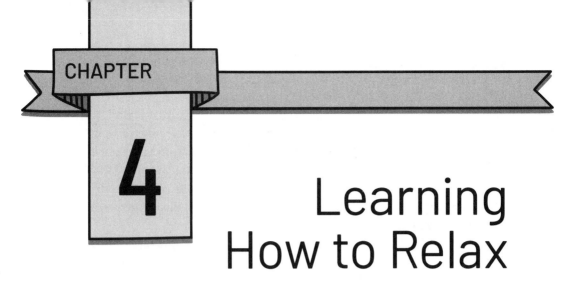

4

Learning How to Relax

"Learning how to be able to sit and relax took a while for me. I had to practice every day and mostly listened to relaxing imagery with music in the background. I used to squirm around a lot and keep my eyes open, but now I lie still and keep my eyes closed. Practicing paid off, and now I know how to calm down and really relax."

—Ben, age 12

To help you prepare for facing your fears and taking the steps on your ladder, this chapter will teach you several different relaxation techniques. These techniques are also useful for overall stress management. Most people can benefit from learning them. This chapter addresses the "body" part of anxiety, or the physical symptoms of stress and discomfort that are linked to your OCD.

Some kids and teens have a hard time with recognizing when their bodies feel stressed or anxious. As discussed in Chapter 1, common body symptoms include the following:

> muscle tension,
> fast heartbeat,
> sweaty palms,
> shallow breathing (breathing that only goes in your upper chest instead of traveling all the way down to your lower belly),
> stomachaches,
> headaches,
> feeling dizzy or lightheaded,
> hot flushes, and
> feeling restless and panicky.

There are other physical symptoms that could be associated with anxiety from OCD, and every person's body is different.

It is important to know that there is a mind-body connection, meaning that your mind affects your body and your body affects your mind. For example, if the fire alarm goes off at school, your mind registers the alarm and thinks, "Fire! I better get outside!" This causes your body to have a fight-or-flight reaction as it prepares either to run or to protect itself. When this happens, your heartbeat gets fast, blood flows into your legs, and your body temperature rises. Your body and mind work together and influence one another. Similarly, if you have a positive attitude about your body and your health, you will likely get sick less often. If you worry about your health and think of your body as fragile, you may be more likely to get hurt or injured. Many times, if you *think* it, your body will *feel* it.

Understanding this mind-body connection is important because it relates to your OCD. When your OCD is triggered, your mind is registering that there is a threat or something to be worried or alerted about, and then your body will have a hard time being relaxed. The steps on your ladder represent difficult situations that you tend to avoid, and you likely avoid them because they are so unpleasant and uncomfortable for you.

Also, you probably don't *feel* that good when in those situations. Right now, because you have spent a long time either avoiding those situations or dealing with them while feeling distressed, those situations have been associated with discomfort and anxiety for you. So, whenever you try to face those situations, it will be hard to do at first. Relaxation is one way that will help you cope, or deal with, the discomfort that you feel when facing your fears, and staying in the situation.

mind-body connection: your mind affects your body and your body affects your mind

Sometimes you will be able to actually relax in such situations, although this will probably not happen during the first few times you practice. Sometimes, however, you will feel so uncomfortable that the purpose of relaxation will simply be to help you better handle or deal with the discomfort, rather than getting completely calm.

The most important thing to keep in mind is that you need to first practice these relaxation techniques while you are relatively calm, not when you are upset or anxious. The goal is to really learn how to relax and become a master at relaxing, so that when you are anxious, you will be able to calm down. If you practice only during times of anxiety, the relaxation may not work as well.

There are several ways to calm the body, and this chapter will focus on five:

1. calm breathing,
2. progressive muscle relaxation,
3. relaxing imagery,
4. mindfulness meditation, and
5. yoga.

The best approach is to practice them all, and then pick one or two that work best for you and use those during the exposure phase. You can practice on your own or have your parent help you in the process if you like. Try to practice calm breathing every day, and then add one of the other techniques, trying a different technique each day until you figure out which one(s) work best for you.

Calm Breathing

Calm breathing is a great technique, and most kids love it. There are two types:

1. lower diaphragmatic breathing (traditional calm breathing), and
2. one-nostril breathing.

Lower Diaphragmatic Breathing (Traditional Calm Breathing)

Your diaphragm is a sheet of muscle wall located just under your ribs, and it is a major muscle used during breathing. "Lower diaphragmatic breathing" refers to breathing in which the breath goes all the way down into the lower part of stomach, below your diaphragm. The goal is for the air to travel all the way down into the lower part of your belly, near your belly button. When you are nervous or scared, your breath only goes into the top of your chest, but when you are calm or relaxed, your breath travels farther down into your lower abdomen.

> **lower diaphragmatic breathing:** breathing in which the breath goes all the way down into the lower part of your stomach, below your diaphragm

The best way to practice this is to lie down on the floor, with a book or a foam block like the ones used in yoga on your chest. Gently breathe in (inhale) through your nose for about 4 seconds and then slowly breathe out (exhale) through your nose for 6 seconds. You want the exhale breath to be longer than the inhale breath.

When you are lying down, imagine that the top of your chest is the shallow end of the pool and that the bottom of your stomach, near your belly button, is the deep end of the pool. You want the air to travel all the way down into the deep end, without causing the shallow end (or the book or block) to rise. Look down at your belly and try to get the breath to "balloon out" the lower part of it. Don't push out the lower part—let the breath cause it to rise and fall. Remember to breathe in and out very slowly.

With the book or block still on your chest, pretend to breathe in an anxious way, only in your upper chest, and watch it move up and down. Now, keep practicing until you are able to keep the book or block consistently still by doing lower diaphragmatic breathing and letting the air go all the way down to your lower stomach—the block will stay still, but your lower belly will rise and fall as you slowly breathe in and out.

If you are having a hard time doing this type of breathing, try using a 10-pound sandbag (another type of yoga prop) and put that on your upper chest instead. Because it weighs so much, the sandbag will make it very hard for you to breathe with your upper chest. It will make you breathe in a calm way. Instead of a sandbag, you could use a big bag of rice. If you do this, ask your parent or other adult for assistance.

Many kids who come to see me have "learned" calm breathing in the past, yet when I ask them to show me, I see that they really haven't learned how to do it correctly. It requires practice, and by using the props (block/book, sandbag/bag of rice), you will really understand what to do. With practice, you will be able to know when your breathing is calm versus when it is anxious.

One-Nostril Breathing

One-nostril breathing is a favorite technique of many of my clients. It forces your body to have a slow, calm breath. The goal is to do this kind of breathing for 3–5 minutes. When you do it for a full 3–5 minutes, you will really start to see the benefits.

Use your finger to hold one of your nostrils closed, and then close your mouth. Breathe very, very slowly in and out through only one nostril.

First, breathe in through one nostril for 5 seconds, then out through the same nostril for 7 seconds. Do this several times to get used to it. Then, do it again, taking 8 seconds to breathe in and 10 seconds to breathe out. Keep this pace for 5 minutes and then see how relaxed you feel.

You can breathe in and out through the same nostril or breathe in through one nostril and then switch and breathe out through the other. The most important part is that you are breathing in or breathing out through only one nostril at a time (while closing the other nostril and keeping your mouth closed). Also, a lot of kids find it helpful to let out a big breath (sort of like a very deep sigh or like you are a balloon deflating) right before they start the calm breathing, as this allows them to have more air to breathe in through their nostril.

Progressive Muscle Relaxation

Progressive muscle relaxation (PMR) involves making your muscles relax by first tightening them up and holding them for about 5–10 seconds, then releasing and relaxing them. You do one section of your body at a time, starting with your hands and going all the way down to your feet. When you use the steps below, pay attention to what your body feels like when your muscles are tight and tense and when they are loose and relaxed.

> **progressive muscle relaxation (PMR):** making your muscles relax by first tightening them up and holding them for about 5–10 seconds, then letting them relax again

Find a comfortable place to sit, and do the following 10 steps:

1. **Hands:** Make tight fists, imagining that you are squeezing the juice out of a lemon. Hold your fists nice and tight and count to 10. Then, let go and shake them out to loosen them up.

2. **Arms:** Now pull your arms into your body, almost pushing them into your ribs. Tighten up your biceps, triceps, and forearm muscles (all of the muscles in your arms above and below your elbows), but don't make fists or tighten your hands. Hold it for 10 seconds, and then let go and shake your arms out. Remember to notice what the muscles feel like when they are tense and when they are loose. Sometimes, once you loosen them, your muscles will feel a little tingly. This is totally normal.

3. **Shoulders:** Bring your shoulders all the way up toward your ears and tighten them up. This also should make the back of your neck tight. Hold it for the count of 10, then allow your shoulders to drop down toward your hips. As you do this, say the word *relax* to yourself and breathe out slowly through your mouth.

4. **Back:** Now, pull your shoulders back and arch your back in toward your chest, trying to get your elbows to touch. Imagine that there is a string connected to your chest and someone is pulling the string up, lifting your chest up toward the ceiling. This will tighten your back. Hold it for 10 seconds, and then let it go and feel the difference between tension and relaxation.

5. **Stomach:** Squeeze and pull your stomach, or abdominal, muscles in toward your spine. Say "hut," like the noise football players make before they snap, or hike, the ball, and hold it in. Keep it tight for 10 seconds, then let it go.

6. **Buttocks:** Now, squeeze your buttocks (muscles in your butt—they are important, too!). Hold for 10 seconds, then let go and loosen them up. Try not to tighten your legs or hamstrings when doing this—just keep it specific to your buttock's muscles.

7. **Legs (toes in):** Stick your legs and feet straight out in front of you and point your toes in toward your chest. This will tighten the muscles in your legs and thighs. Make the muscles as tight as you can and hold for 10 seconds, and then let go and allow your legs to gently drop to the ground and relax.

8. **Legs (toes out):** Stick your legs and feet straight out in front of you again, but this time, point your toes straight out away from you and tighten up the muscles in your legs, thighs, and feet. Try to get it so you feel a little cramping in the bottom of your feet. Hold for 10 seconds, and then let go, allowing your legs to gently drop to the floor.

9. **Face:** Now, tighten up all of the muscles in your face. Start by clenching your teeth and jaw. Then squish up your nose, lifting it up, and then close your eyes and squeeze the muscles around them, tightening up your forehead. Hold this tightness in your whole face for 10 seconds, and then let go and relax. Open your mouth a little bit and move your jaw from left to right and then in circles. This will allow the jaw to become even more relaxed.

10. **Whole body:** You want to go from being a stiff, tight **robot** to being a loose, relaxed **rag doll**! Start with tight fists, then add arms, then bring your shoulders up to your ears, then pull them back to tighten your back, then squeeze your stomach into your spine, then tighten your buttocks, then put your legs out in front of you with your toes pointing away from you and cramp up your feet, and then tighten your jaw and whole face. Hold for 10 seconds (robot) and then let go (rag doll), loosening every muscle in your body. I could tell that you were a really relaxed rag doll if I tried to lift up your arm and it felt very heavy and loose.

Relaxing Imagery

Relaxing imagery is another way to relax your body and mind. There are so many wonderful apps that offer relaxing imagery and guided meditation (more are listed in the Resources section at the back of this book). Here are my three favorite ones:

> Insight Timer,
> Calm, and
> Headspace.

When you listen, find a comfortable place to sit or lie down. You can make yourself more comfortable by using pillows or arranging blankets to have more support under your head and under your knees.

If you'd prefer not to use apps, you can use one of these relaxing imaginal exposure recordings instead. You can either read the scene yourself or have a parent or someone else read it to you. Just make sure that they use their best calming voice and that they don't read it too quickly. I recommend that either you or your parent make a recording of one of the imaginal exposure recordings below, and then you can replay the recording and listen to it regularly.

Here is the first relaxing imagery script.

RELAXING IMAGERY   SCRIPT 1

Once you are comfortable, **close your eyes and take a deep breath in through your nose and out through your mouth.** As you breathe in, imagine that you are breathing in clean, relaxing air, and as you breathe out, let go of any stress or tension that you might be holding onto. Breathing in, let the calm air go all the way down to the bottom of your belly. Breathing out, let go of the air so your belly becomes flat. With each breath, you feel more and more relaxed.

This is your time for relaxation, and you have nowhere to go and nothing to do. If any thoughts come into your mind, that is perfectly fine. Just let them flow by without focusing on them. Anything important will come back to you after the relaxation.

RELAXING IMAGERY   SCRIPT 1, continued

Imagine that you are visiting a beautiful lake, and picture yourself sitting or standing close to the water. Your body feels so comfortable and calm. It is a perfect day and the temperature is just right—not too hot, and there is a soothing breeze that you feel especially on your face. You notice that your body begins to loosen up.

Look at the water—notice how peaceful the water is. You can hear the sound of the water as it hits up against the land. You love the sound that the water makes as it keeps rocking up and down, back and forth, against the land. The rhythm of the water coming in and out toward the land is very soothing, and you notice your attention is locked onto the water. The more you watch the water, the calmer you feel. You begin to feel your muscles loosen and your breathing slow down. You feel very, very calm. Watching the water is soothing and calming.

The breeze is making slight waves on the surface of the water, and you love watching these waves flowing in, then flowing out, and then just flowing along. Nature is very peaceful. You can trust nature, and you feel yourself being held by the beauty around you.

Lying on the grass next to the lake, you think more about these waves. You imagine a wave coming over your body, and as it does, it soothes and comforts you. The wave slowly goes over your toes, feet, and ankles. Then it goes up your legs, knees, and thighs. It goes over your hips, hands, arms, stomach, and chest, and all the way up to your shoulders, just up to your neck. The wave is warm and comforting. It hangs out for just a minute, relaxing and soothing all of your muscles.Then the wave begins to leave, taking away all remaining tension, going down your chest, stomach, arms, hands, and hips, all the way down past your thighs, knees, legs, and ankles, and then finally leaving your feet and toes. You are now even more relaxed, and your body feels light and loose.

RELAXING IMAGERY   SCRIPT 1, continued

Looking back toward the lake, you see magnificent mountains in the distance. The mountains are strong, and you enjoy looking at them and thinking about just how amazing they are. There are some white clouds looming around the tops of the mountains, set against the background of a bright blue sky. Again, you are in a state of deep peace and inner calmness.

(pause for a moment)

You notice the sounds of birds singing and the sounds of the wind blowing, and you love the feeling of being surrounded by nature. You see trees near the lake, and their leaves are swaying back and forth as the breeze comes and goes. Be fully aware of this moment and of all of the things you are seeing, hearing, and feeling. Notice how your body feels. Take a moment to enjoy this relaxation, noticing how calm and slow your breathing is. Stay here as long as you'd like.

(pause for several minutes and enjoy this relaxed state)

In just a minute, count to 10, and imagine that you are climbing up a set of stairs. With each step, you become more and more alert, but still very relaxed. At the top of the stairs, there will be an archway. You will walk through the archway, and then you will be back in your own room, keeping the feelings of relaxation within you.

One, take the first step.
Two, take the second step.
Three, take the third step.
Four, take the fourth step.
Five, take the fifth step.
Six, take the sixth step.
Seven, take the seventh step.
Eight, take the eighth step.

RELAXING IMAGERY   SCRIPT 1, continued

Nine, take the ninth step.
And ten, take the tenth step.

Walk through the archway, and you are back in your room.
Remind yourself that you can become this relaxed anytime you'd
like, and it will only take 5 minutes.

You can practice relaxing imagery with this or any other relaxing
scene. You can ask your parent to make up a scene for you, or you can
create one yourself. It can be anywhere you'd like—it can be a real place,
such as a special place that you have traveled to, one you have seen in a
movie, or a made-up one. The only rule is that this place needs to be free
of stress and completely relaxing to you.

You either can stop here and skip ahead to the section on mindfulness meditation, or you can read through the additional script below.

An alternative relaxing imagery scene follows that you can use
instead of, or in addition to, the lake scene above. Again, either you or
your parent can make a recording for you to listen to when practicing
relaxation.

RELAXING IMAGERY   SCRIPT 2

Once you are comfortable, **close your eyes and take a deep
breath in through your nose and out through your mouth.** As
you breathe in, imagine that you are breathing in clean, relaxing
air, and as you breathe out, let go of any stress or tension that
you might be holding on to. Breathing in, let the calm air go all
the way down to the bottom of your belly. Breathing out, let go
of the air so your belly becomes flat. With each breath, you feel
more and more relaxed.

This is your time for relaxation, and you have nowhere to go
and nothing to do. If any thoughts come into your mind, that is

---

RELAXING IMAGERY   SCRIPT 2, continued

perfectly fine. Just let them flow by without focusing on them. Anything important will come back to you after the relaxation.

Imagine that you are in a beautiful field. This field is a very safe and relaxing place. The field is vast and wide, and you can see everything clearly around you. Part of the field is lined with wheat, and you notice how the wind softly blows the tips of the wheat and how relaxing this is to watch. Another part of the field is a large stretch of green grass, and there are several big, beautiful trees. Two of the trees have a hammock stretched between them.

You look out into the field and notice that your whole body feels calm. You have a feeling of being held and comforted. You can feel the sun shining down upon you, warming your body. The air is the perfect temperature, and the sky is blue with white, cottony clouds.

You move closer to the wheat grass and notice its lovely colors, with the sunlight causing the tips to glisten as they sway from the breeze. The smell is fresh and natural. You run your fingers over the top of the grass, feeling how soft and light it is. You swing both of your hands out in front of you, along the top edges of the grass. You are standing tall, but relaxed. You feel lightness and confidence in your body. You feel clear in your body, free of tension. You close your eyes for a moment, feeling the sunlight warming your face. You breathe in and out calmly and become even more relaxed.

(pause for a moment)

Looking at the trees, you are reminded of how strong the Earth is. You can imagine the roots of the trees and how far down they go, securing their position in the Earth. You feel the strength of the trees, and this makes you feel safe and secure. You walk toward the trees and decide to settle into the hammock. Sitting down, you swing one leg up onto the hammock and then the

RELAXING IMAGERY   SCRIPT 2, continued

other. This hammock is so comfortable and relaxing. You lie back and your body sways from left to right, left to right. You look up at the tops of the trees and see the leaves swaying from the wind. You hear birds in the background, including an owl— whooo, whooo, whooo. You love how the owl sounds, and you are so relaxed that you gently close your eyes and just enjoy the calm swaying back and forth, back and forth. Sunlight streams through the tops of the trees and moves through the leaves and branches, causing patches of sunlight to rest upon your body, providing you with additional warmth. You are so content. You are so calm.

(pause for a moment)

Be fully aware of this moment, and all of the things you are seeing, hearing, and feeling. Notice how your body feels. Take a moment to enjoy this relaxation, noticing how calm and slow your breathing is. Stay here as long as you'd like.

(pause for several minutes and enjoy relaxed state)

In just a minute, count to 10, and imagine that you are climbing up a set of stairs. With each step, you become more and more alert, but still very relaxed. At the top of the stairs, there will be an archway. You will walk through the archway, and then you will be back in your own room, keeping the feelings of relaxation within you.

One, take the first step.
Two, take the second step.
Three, take the third step.
Four, take the fourth step.
Five, take the fifth step.
Six, take the sixth step.
Seven, take the seventh step.
Eight, take the eighth step.

RELAXING IMAGERY   SCRIPT 2, continued

Nine, take the ninth step.
And ten, take the tenth step.

Walk through the archway, and you are back in your room.
Remind yourself that you can become this relaxed anytime you'd
like, and it will only take 5 minutes!

Mindfulness Meditation

Of all of the different ways to relax your body and mind, meditation is very useful in helping you "stay with" the uncomfortable feelings of anxiety, which is important to be able to do when doing the exposures. There are many different types of meditation. The one you will learn here is called "mindfulness meditation."

The term *mindfulness* was introduced to you in Chapter 2, where it was explained that mindfulness refers to a different way of experiencing yourself and the mind. It involves being fully aware in the present moment, the exact moment that you are in right now. When you can truly be in the present moment, you will see that you are totally okay. No matter what you might be upset about from the past, or what you are worried about for the future, you are completely fine in the present moment. Nothing bad is happening to you in this moment. Even though anxiety might make you *feel* this way (because anxiety signals a threat), nothing bad is actually happening to you.

Mindfulness is being fully aware of yourself and your thoughts, but in a way that allows you to be less reactive to them. For example, you might notice that you are feeling anxious and are uncomfortable, yet by *noticing* it, you will tend to be a bit separated, or distanced, from it, and then will be less likely to *react* to it. It is as if you become an observer of your anxiety and discomfort.

When dealing with OCD, the goal is to be fully aware of when you are being triggered into OCD thoughts and what those thoughts are. It is easy to feel that the OCD is just the way you are or is just a typical part of your life. Being mindful will allow you to be more aware of your OCD, how it comes out in your life, and how it makes you feel.

The concept of mindfulness is now regularly being integrated into schools and the curriculum, so it might not be new to you. Learning how to *be mindful* is the fundamental skill of mindfulness meditation. When you are mindful, you are really experiencing the present moment, and this is necessary when practicing meditation.

The more often you practice, the more it will start to come naturally to you. Some kids will find it pretty easy to get out of their thinking mind, while others will find it very difficult and will need more practice. Either way, just be confident that you will be able to achieve this skill. Try not to judge yourself or the process itself. There is no such thing as "doing it right" because it's not about doing anything. Rather, it's about simply being. Start with a 5–10-minute practice session each day (right before bed is a great time because you want to wind down anyway, and this practice will help), and gradually build up to a longer practice, such as 20–30 minutes.

MINDFULNESS MEDITATION PRACTICE

Find a comfortable place to sit or lie down. You can choose to close your eyes or keep them open. Focus your attention on the present moment. Just "be" in the moment that you are in. This is not something that should feel like effort, or like something you are trying to do. Instead, allow your natural state of being just to happen. You were born into a state of awareness and full consciousness, so by doing this, you are really going back to basics.

If you find yourself thinking of something, just note that you are having a thought, and allow yourself to move on. Allow the thought to float on by—don't hold onto it or push it away—just let it float on by you.

Bring your focus to your breath. Feel your lower belly and how it goes up and down with each incoming and outgoing breath. Ground yourself in your breath. Now extend your awareness throughout your body. Feel the support of the chair or the floor below you. Be fully aware of your body.

MINDFULNESS MEDITATION PRACTICE, continued

Now extend your awareness to the space around you. Feel the energy of the space in the room you are in and extend your awareness throughout the room.

Now expand your awareness to outside of the room. Imagine that you are spreading your awareness to beyond the room, into the outside space around you.

Notice the sounds and vibrations around you. Allow those sounds to become a part of your field of awareness. Just observe what you observe.

Again, if any thoughts come into your mind, just let them pass. Don't do anything with them—don't hold onto them or try to push them away. Just stay with the moment you are in. Just sit there in awareness, letting yourself simply be in your natural state.

Note: When doing this, it may feel like you are doing nothing, and to some extent, that is exactly what you are doing. However, the practice of doing nothing and having a clear mind allows you to experience anxiety-free states and know what it feels like to not be consumed with OCD thoughts.

Yoga

Yoga is a form of exercise that greatly helps your body and mind. In fact, the word *yoga* means "to join" or "to unite." There are many different types of yoga, but the goal of most types is to help you gain more balance and strength in your body and bring harmony to your body and mind. Research shows that yoga is beneficial for improving anxiety, stress, and depression.

Taking a yoga class or watching a yoga video is the best way to learn the poses and to make sure you do them correctly without getting injured. There are countless options on YouTube and other websites.

Below are three popular poses that are pretty easy to learn and very safe to do. The more you practice, the better you will become at getting the most out of these poses.

1. Standing Mountain Pose

Stand with your feet together (big toes touching) and your arms down by your sides. Stand up nice and tall and very straight with your shoulders back. Try to get your chest to lift up, as if someone is pulling your chest up with a string that is attached to it.

1. Now, turn your palms facing out, away from you. Slowly raise your arms, keeping your elbows straight if you can. Once your arms are all the way up, your hands will be facing one another, and your fingers will be reaching up toward the sky.
2. Stretch up and reach up as high as you can, while keeping your feet planted firmly into the floor. Try to encourage your upper spine to move into your body and your shoulder blades to move closer together.
3. Continue to reach up with your fingertips, and push your feet down into the floor, as if your feet were the roots of a tree (your leg muscles should become tight as you do this). Your upper body is stretching up while your lower body is pushing down. As you do this, feel confident about yourself and feel your body opening and lengthening as you stretch and stretch.

2. Downward-Facing Dog Pose

Lie face down on the floor, bend your elbows, and put your hands down on the floor next to your armpits (or chest).

1. Now, get up on all fours (on your hands and knees) and spread your fingers apart, but keep your hands with open palms on the floor.
2. Now, lift up onto your feet, standing mainly on your toes, lifting your hips up, and keeping your hands on the floor. Your hands should be shoulder-width apart.

3. Continue to lift your hips up and stretch your back. Continue to spread your fingers apart and push your hands against the floor to encourage more lengthening in your spine and more lift in your hips. Hips up, hips up. Try to bring the spine into the body. Feel the stretch.

4. Very good! Now, gently come back down onto all fours, lie back down on your stomach, and relax.

3. Child's Pose

Lie face down on the floor and touch your big toes together while sitting on the heels of your feet.

1. Now, spread your knees apart so your knees go out toward the side.

2. Lay your chest on the floor and let your belly sink down toward the floor as well. Your thighs and knees should be out to the side.

3. Stretch your arms and fingers out in front of you with your arms lifting up a few inches above the floor and your fingertips touching the floor. As you do this, try to get your upper back and upper spine to come into your body. Feel the stretch.

4. Now, bring your arms down by your sides, with your hands (palms facing up) resting on the floor alongside or below your feet. Just let your entire body relax and rest. Let go of any tension in your body.

What I Know Now

This chapter focused on teaching you several different ways to relax. You learned calm breathing, including lower diaphragmatic breathing and one-nostril breathing, progressive muscle relaxation, relaxing imagery, mindfulness meditation, and several yoga poses. Each of these techniques was explained, and you are reminded to practice each technique, with the goal of identifying one or two that work really well and will be useful for you during the exposure/practice phase.

5

Challenging Obsessive Thoughts and Worries, PART 1

"It was hard to struggle with OCD and all my OCD thoughts that made me doubt everything. I felt unsure of everything and even had a hard time answering simple questions that my friends would ask. Once I figured out how to talk back to my OCD and make myself answer anyway—even when I didn't feel sure—things started to get better."

—Sydney, age 10

Although all of the chapters in this book are important in helping you take control of OCD, this chapter and the next one are the most necessary to your success in doing so. This chapter focuses on helping you challenge the thoughts and worries that come from OCD. The next chapter focuses on challenging OCD thoughts and worries through the use of loop and imaginal exposure recordings. Therefore, this and the next chapter are about the *thoughts* part of OCD.

The following is a list of the strategies you will learn that address the "cognitive" or thoughts part of OCD:

> OCD cycle,
> "When my OCD talks, it says . . .",
> "Stamping" it "OCD",
> positive self-talk,
> distraction,
> thinking errors and cognitive restructuring,
> thoughts challenge form,
> detached mindfulness,
> attention training technique,
> loop recordings (Chapter 6), and
> imaginal exposure recordings (Chapter 6).

OCD Cycle

In review of the OCD cycle, there is an event (trigger situation) followed by an obsessive thought (which tends to be a thinking error or other unrealistic assessment of the situation), and then the person feels anxious or upset. To cope with the anxiety, there is a compulsive behavior or ritual (action). Obsessive thoughts can come up in many forms, including repetitive ideas, doubts, questioning, and disturbing images.

The reason it is important to know the OCD cycle is that it allows you to understand the process that leads to doing compulsions. When you see the cycle happening, you can interrupt it. By understanding that you have to intercept it by challenging the thoughts and intercept it again by challenging the compulsive behavior, you will be better able to do this when you see the thoughts and behavior as part of a cycle that keeps the OCD going. Also, knowing that OCD happens in a cycle allows you to "externalize" the OCD, which is when you can see it as separate from yourself (external to you, rather than part of you, which is internal). Another way to do this is to know what your OCD sounds like, which is the next strategy.

Identifying Your OCD Thoughts: When My OCD Talks, It Says . . .

It is important to identify your own OCD-driven thoughts, not only to externalize the OCD, but also to know what thoughts to challenge. As explained in Chapter 2, externalizing the OCD means that you clearly see what OCD is causing you to think. Therefore, you see it as something separate from yourself: Rather than considering the OCD thoughts to be just your own thoughts, you are able to identify those thoughts as symptoms of the disorder.

To help you complete the section below, let's go through a few of the examples of children and teens with OCD to show how they completed the exercise on identifying their OCD thoughts.

Andrew, 12 Years Old: Contamination Type

When Andrew's OCD talked, it said . . .
> "Bathrooms are dangerous, and there are dangerous germs in there."
> "If I touch the toilet, I will get contaminated and sick."
> "If I touch the faucet, I will get someone's germs and might not know it."
> "I can prevent getting sick if I am very careful when using bathrooms."
> "You have to go through the whole alphabet to wash your hands well enough."
> "It is dangerous to be near people who are sick."

Sydney, 10 Years Old: Doubting/Indecisiveness Types

When Sydney's OCD talked, it said . . .
> "What if I stepped on a pencil?"
> "If I tell Mom everything I did, then I will feel better."

> "I should only wear clothes that feel completely right to wear."
> "I shouldn't make a mistake."
> "There is a right decision and a wrong decision. I will know it's right when it feels right to me."
> "I shouldn't upset my friends or disappoint anyone."
> "What if the toilet paper touched the floor in the bathroom?"
> "What if I stepped on an animal? I felt like I stepped on something. I better go back and check."

William, 16 Years Old: Scrupulosity Type

When William's OCD talked, it said . . .
> "Having fun increases the chances that I will be punished."
> "Something bad will happen if I enjoy myself and feel pleasure."
> "It is safer to stay home and do homework."
> "I have to be careful and not take risks. I need to be in control."
> "I shouldn't go out on school nights."
> "Scheduling or organizing plans with friends makes it worse. Then I am responsible for the fun. It's better if someone else arranges the plans."

Lina, 13 Years Old: Sexual Orientation Type

When Lina's OCD talked, it said . . .
> "Why are you looking at her?"
> "Do you have feelings for her? You must because you keep looking!"
> "What if you are a lesbian? Do you even know who you are?"
> "Why are you so afraid of being a lesbian? Maybe you are homophobic."
> "This is how lesbians realize they are lesbian."
> "If you are having doubts that you are straight, you probably aren't."
> "Even though people will accept you, you never know."
> "If you spend time with her, you probably will realize you are a lesbian."
> "If you go out with that boy, you probably will know you are a lesbian."

Talia, 17 Years Old: Hypochondria/Health Type

When Talia's OCD talked, it said . . .
> "I shouldn't feel this tired; there is obviously something wrong."
> "What if I have leukemia? What if I die this year?"
> "How will my family be okay if I die?"
> "I should probably get this checked out to be on the safe side."
> "Maybe it's not anxiety but is a premonition that something bad will happen to me."
> "Maybe I have this anxiety because it will make me go to the doctor because something really is wrong with me."
> "If I wear these clothes, something will happen."
> "How could you deal with knowing you are going to die."
> "What if I am sick and going to die and no one is telling me?"

Using the "When My OCD Talks, It Says . . ." worksheet or on a separate sheet of paper, make a list of what your OCD says when it is triggered.

When my OCD talks, it says . . .

"Stamping" It "OCD"

Similar to the OCD cycle and "When my OCD talks, it says . . .", using this strategy called "Stamping" it "OCD" allows you to externalize the OCD and see it as separate from yourself. By externalizing it, you are better able to interrupt it and resist it. I often think of getting caught up in the OCD as "getting in the boat" rather than staying on the dock. When you are triggered by OCD, it's like you are suddenly stuck in a rocky boat in the water. By externalizing the OCD, you can see it as OCD, rather than getting caught up in the cycle. The goal is to stay on the dock, where it's stable and you are not feeling threatened, and see the OCD as the rocky boat without getting in it. Detached mindfulness, which is described toward the end of this chapter, offers another way to do this.

"Stamping" it "OCD" involves writing several of your OCD thoughts in random order on different parts of a sheet of paper, leaving space between each. Using a red or black marker, "stamp" each thought by writing "OCD" over the thought, in big, thick letters. When the thick red or black ink is written over the thought, it becomes hard to read what it says. Many kids and teens have found this helpful, and then when they have a random OCD thought come up, they visualize "stamping" it with a big OCD stamp, allowing them to be able to dismiss the thought and not get caught up in what the thought is about. The goal is not to try to forget about the thought, but to be able to see it as only a symptom of OCD, which makes it easy to separate from and not be impacted by.

The "Stamping It OCD" graphic shows what it looks like to "stamp" something "OCD," using Sydney's thoughts.

self-talk: what you say to yourself; when you are feeling anxious or triggered by OCD, your self-talk is negative

Positive Self-Talk: Talking Back to the OCD

Self-talk is what you say to yourself. When you are feeling anxious or triggered by OCD, your self-talk is negative. An example of negative

self-talk is, "I can't handle this. It's better to keep washing my hands until the OCD feels okay." One goal in challenging your thoughts is to change your self-talk, making it more positive and empowering. Changing your self-talk is another way of challenging OCD and preventing compulsions, and you definitely want to use positive self-talk when you are doing the exposures. Below are examples of positive self-talk. Try to identify about 10 of them that will be useful for you and write each one on a note card:

> I must face my fears to overcome them. I can do it.
> I am uncomfortable and I can handle it.
> I'm scared and I am safe.
> In the present moment, I am okay. Everything is fine.
> I can handle this.
> I can change the way I think to change the way I feel.
> I am uncomfortable, but I am fine.
> I can tolerate the discomfort that comes from facing my OCD.
> Anxiety is not an accurate predictor of what's to come. It's just an unpleasant feeling.
> I can help myself relax. Let me do my calm breathing.
> What would someone without OCD think? What would they do?
> It is just the OCD talking. Someone without OCD wouldn't be having this thought. I don't have to listen to the OCD.
> It's me versus the OCD. Each time I listen to the OCD, it becomes stronger, and each time I don't, I become stronger. I must handle the temporary anxiety that comes when I do not give in.
> I cannot let OCD make decisions for me or control my life.
> I cannot allow OCD to influence my behavior or my family's behavior.
> Doing these rituals isn't working; it's just keeping the OCD around longer.
> I've never regretted facing my fears.
> Once I prevent or even delay the ritual, after a few minutes, the urge is gone and I'm fine. The hardest part is not giving in at first.
> Thoughts have no power unless I give them power. Thoughts are just thoughts.
> I can become an observer of my thoughts rather than a participant in them. I can see that it's "just a thought."
> I have to disconnect from the content of my OCD thoughts. I must see them and label them as "symptoms of OCD" rather than real thoughts deserving of consideration.
> I have to "sit with" and tolerate the discomfort that comes from not giving in to the OCD.

> This is about tolerating negative emotions. I can handle whatever I feel. I don't need to be overwhelmed by what I feel.
> I have to tolerate the uncertainty of the situation and how I cannot know for sure. Some uncertainty is part of the normal life experience.
> This is about changing my relationship with my thoughts. I have to expect that the thoughts will come up in my trigger situation. I will plan for how to respond to it without giving in.
> Courage comes after slaying the dragon. Once I face my fears, I will realize that I can do it.

Distraction

When OCD triggers come up and you get stuck, it may be hard to use any of the strategies, so distraction can be useful as a temporary strategy. The same is true if the exposure/response prevention (ERP) is too activating and making you too anxious, and you need to temporarily focus on something else. You can use distraction to take your attention away from the worry and put your focus on something else. Once calmer, you can return to using the CBT strategies or doing the ERP practices. It is very important, however, that you **do not** use distraction when you are doing the exposures, as that will just be a form of avoidance. For example, if you are eating food you usually avoid due to fears of contamination and start to use distraction during it to "get through" it, you won't actually benefit from the exposure. **For the exposure to work, you need to experience the discomfort that comes from doing the practice and tolerating it until you get used to it (which *will* happen).**

Distraction occupies the mind and gives the body the chance to slow down and be calmer. You can also use distraction to prevent rumination (when your thoughts go in a spiral, and you get stuck on particular thoughts, going over them again and again).

distraction: doing something to take your attention away from the worry and temporarily bring your focus to something else

Here are some distraction techniques:
> Use the alphabet to come up with lists, for example:
>> Boys' names: Andre, Brian, Cole, David, Evan, Fred, Gabe, Henry, Isaac
>> Girls' names: Anna, Bonnie, Camryn, Dahlia, Emily, Frances, Grace, Helena, Ivory
>> Jobs: artist, baker, chemist, dentist, engineer, financial analyst, geographer, horticulturist, inventor
>> Cities/states/countries: Aventura, Bethesda, Chicago, Denmark, Ecuador, Florida, Guam, Honduras

> Make your own lists, such as five things that are green, five things in my backpack, my five favorite songs or movies.
> Play a game or do a puzzle.

The distraction techniques should be easy to use and not require much work. Again, they are used for just a short period of time before doing the hard work of ERP or calming yourself down so you can better use the CBT strategies or to prevent rumination.

Thinking Mistakes (Also Called "Cognitive Distortions")

Everyone makes thinking mistakes, or cognitive errors, particularly when they are anxious. For example, some people are afraid to fly in an airplane and either avoid flying or are very nervous when they fly. These people think flying is dangerous, and they worry that if they fly, they will die in a plane crash. This type of thinking is a thinking error called "catastrophizing." It is a thinking error because flying is not dangerous. That conclusion is based on fear, not on reality. In fact, flying is the safest form of transportation and is very safe in general. Although planes do crash, the large majority of the time, they do not. In fact, one's chances of dying in a plane crash are 1 in 11 million. This is a very, very low risk, and one's chances of winning the lottery are actually better! Therefore, being on a plane often is the *safest* place to be! Catastrophizing is when someone uses "what if . . ." thinking, ends up thinking about the worst-case scenario, and often acts as if the disaster will happen. When working to overcome anxiety, a person needs to identify and replace their thinking errors.

People with OCD make thinking errors. The goal is to figure out which ones you tend to use. Identifying your thinking errors and learning how to replace them with more balanced, realistic thoughts is another strategy to challenge the OCD. There are many different types of thinking errors, and the following is a list of the ones most often used in OCD.

Types of Thinking Errors

1. **Catastrophizing:** Visualizing disaster, thinking that the worst thing is going to happen, and feeling like you wouldn't be able to handle it; asking "What if . . .?"
   > Example: What if the cookies were cooked with bad eggs and I get salmonella poisoning?
   > Example: What if I touch the toilet seat and get AIDS?

2. **All-or-nothing:** Thinking in extremes, meaning that things are either perfect or a failure; there is no middle ground—it's either one extreme or another; thinking in an inflexible way.
   > Example: My shoes have to be completely organized in my closet, or else my whole closet is not neat and not organized.
   > Example: Going out on a school night is bad. I will only let myself go out on weekends.

3. **Superstitious thinking:** Thinking that by doing something, you will cause or prevent something else from happening.
   > Example: "If I tell my parents I love them three times before bed, we will all be safe. If I don't say goodnight in the right order, something bad might happen."
   > Example: "If I knock on wood whenever I have a bad thought, then nothing bad will happen to me."

4. **Magical thinking:** Thinking some things are lucky and some things are unlucky, such as numbers.
   > Example: "The number four is lucky, so I will buy the fourth magazine, use the fourth tissue, and knock on wood four times."

> Example: "There are good signs and bad signs. If I hear a certain song, I know that it's a bad sign and something bad will happen, so I should turn off the radio."

5. **Selective attention:** Paying attention to information that confirms your beliefs; ignoring evidence that goes against what you believe.
   > Example: Food can be dangerous and cause you to die. Several foods were on recall last year, and many people got salmonella and other diseases from eating contaminated meat.
   > Example: Bathrooms are dirty places, especially doorknobs. I remember that one time a man used the toilet and then didn't wash his hands and touched the doorknob.

6. **Magnifying:** Making something seem bigger and worse than it really is; turning up the volume on anything bad, making it worse.
   > Example: You have a cough and feel sick and start to think about missing school and the work you will miss and how it will be impossible to catch up.
   > Example: When your dad parallel-parked the car, he lightly bumped the car behind him and you got very upset, called it an accident, and wanted to leave a note.

7. **Shoulds:** Having rules about how things should be; using the words *should*, *must*, and *ought to* in order to show how things should be.
   > Example: You make a mistake and forget to hand in an assignment. When you hand it in the next day, your teacher marks it down to a "B" because it is late. You feel so upset with yourself and think, "I shouldn't make mistakes like this. That was so stupid of me."
   > Example: I shouldn't upset or disappoint my friends. Others should think only good things about me.

8. **Thought-action fusion:** Believing that if you have a thought or an urge to do something, then it will cause you to do it.
   > Example: If I have the thought about hurting my brother, then that means I will do it.
   > Example: If I think that I will forget to turn off the stove, then it means I will end up leaving it on.

9. **Thought-event fusion:** Believing that if you have the thought about something happening, then it will cause it to happen or means it already happened.
   > Example: If I have an image of stepping on an animal and killing it, then this means I did and should go back and check.
   > Example: If I have the thought about stabbing someone, then it means that will happen (even though I don't want it to).

10. **Overvaluing thoughts:** This is similar to the fusion beliefs, and it's when you think your thoughts are an accurate measure of who you really are or of your true intentions.
    > Example: If I have a bad thought about hurting children, then it means I'm a bad person.
    > Example: My thoughts are coming from me and are a true reflection of who I really am.

Once you have identified which thinking errors you make, the next step is to practice challenging them and replacing them with more realistic thoughts. The goal is to come up with balanced, neutral thoughts, rather than positive ones. For example, instead of thinking that you will get sick from eating yogurt that expired yesterday, you can think that most likely you will not get sick and that the expiration date is not an exact calculation. You also can think that many people eat yogurt that expired yesterday without getting sick. For example, instead of thinking that going out on school nights is wrong, you might challenge that idea and ask yourself, "What is really wrong about it? What would I do instead of going out? Is going out any different than watching TV at home?" For example, instead of thinking that you can't do work unless everything on your desk is aligned and in order, try reading one paragraph of your book while things are out of order, just to see if you are capable of reading while things are not perfect on your desk.

To replace your thoughts, you want to "consider the facts" and ask yourself, "What proof do I have that this thought is correct?" For example, what proof do you have that you will get AIDS from using a public bathroom? What proof do you have that going out on a weekday is bad or wrong, or that it will lead to punishment? What proof do you have that eating cookies is dangerous? Although I discourage searching the web for answers (usually because someone with OCD or anxiety will use selective attention to find information that confirms their anxious beliefs), it can be useful, particularly if your parent or therapist assists you, to do an information-gathering search from respectable and reputable sites to get the facts. For example, Andrew and I did a search on methods of getting HIV/AIDS because during his treatment, he shared that he was afraid that he could get AIDS from using a public bathroom. We looked on reputable sites (like those ending in .gov) and also referred to the Whitman-Walker Health website and found useful information on how someone can contract AIDS (and by the way, you cannot get AIDS from using a public bathroom). Gathering the facts was helpful for Andrew, and he used the information to challenge his catastrophic fears and OCD thoughts.

Challenge your anxious thoughts by asking yourself, "What would someone without OCD think in this situation?" or "What would someone who is not anxious in this situation think right now?" Consider what a positive outcome might look like. I can tell you countless examples of situations in which the worst-case scenario could have happened, and it didn't. For example, one day I came home to find that the gas stove in my kitchen was completely on, and it had been on for several hours while no one was home! Someone had mistakenly left it on, and the flame had been on for hours, with no bad outcome. There was no fire, no danger, and nothing was wrong. I also know of many people who have left candles burning in their homes by mistake, and nothing bad happened. Dr. Mary Alvord, a well-respected psychologist with whom I have worked, told me that years ago, she and her family went on vacation for 2 weeks and someone forgot to lock their front door. So here they were, out of the state for 2 weeks with the front door of their house left unlocked, and nothing happened—no burglars broke in, and no one stole anything! Their house was totally fine. These stories are good reminders that even when there is potential for a problem, it doesn't mean that a problem will occur. Much of the time, things work out just fine.

Another useful strategy to challenge your thinking errors is to write down your thoughts in a journal. You can make three columns: one for your automatic thought, one to label the thinking error you used, and one to write a new, balanced thought to replace it. Alternatively, you can use the Thoughts Challenge Form described next.

Thoughts Challenge Form

Reframing your OCD thoughts and your worries by finding a different way of thinking about them is a main goal of overcoming OCD. For example, a client with obsessive worries had a fear of having an allergic reaction to nuts, even though he was not allergic at all. He avoided nuts and would ruminate for hours after meals (especially after eating in a restaurant or at someone else's home), worrying that he might have eaten nuts without knowing it and would have an allergic reaction. In challenging his worries, he learned to remind himself that he was not allergic (realistic thinking) and told himself that he could've picked lettuce to be afraid of (because that was another food that he was not allergic to but one he was not afraid of). Then, during the exposure phase when he was eating nuts, he told himself, "It's just lettuce. To my body, it's the same as if I was eating lettuce." This kind of cognitive reframe, also called "cognitive restructuring," helped him undo and weaken his worries and also allowed him to do the exposures and not let the worries control his behavior.

The goal in challenging your thoughts is to figure out which thinking error(s) you are using and come up with alternative beliefs. A main way to do this is to think about what evidence there is to support the belief, and what evidence goes against it.

Sometimes it will be useful to complete a form that guides you on how to challenge your OCD thoughts and beliefs and helps to disrupt the OCD cycle. The "Thoughts Challenge Form" is one that you can use. You can make copies and use it each time you are triggered.

Detached Mindfulness

The detached mindfulness technique, which is part of metacognitive therapy, was introduced in Chapter 2 and helps you to identify your worries as "just thoughts." This allows you to see that whatever you are thinking about, whether it is true or not, is just a thought. For example, when Alicia would think, "I will get salmonella and throw up," she used detached mindfulness and told herself, "That is just a thought. I see that it is just a thought, just like reading is just reading, running is just run-

Thoughts Challenge Form

Event or triggering situation (What caused the OCD to get set off?):

Automatic thought(s), images, or urges (What are you thinking or imagining, or what do you believe?):

How much do you believe the thought? (On a scale of 0–10, with 0 being not at all and 10 being completely true; or you can write in "a little," "medium," or "a great deal"):

Rate how anxious you are (On a scale of 0–10, with 0 being not anxious at all and 10 being the most anxious):

What thinking errors might you be using?:

What is a more realistic way of thinking about it? What would someone without OCD think?:

ning, thinking is just thinking. Thinking is just thinking. No matter what I am thinking about, it is still *only* thinking. And because it is only thinking, I can put off checking right now." She also told herself that thoughts have no power.

In detached mindfulness, you don't try to actually change the thought—you just try to change how you experience the thought, making it something you can observe yourself doing, rather than something you respond to. The goal is to become an "observer" of your thoughts, rather than a participant in them. With practice, this will be a skill you have command of, although at first it might seem hard to do. Once you figure out how to do it, it will come more naturally and easily.

To learn detached mindfulness, write 10 different thoughts on 10 different sheets of paper. Of the 10 thoughts, make seven of them neutral, non-anxiety/non-OCD thoughts (N), make two of them OCD thoughts (OCD), and one of them an untrue thought (U). Once you write them out, mix them together, putting them in the following order: N, N, N, OCD, N, N, U, N, OCD, N. Here is an example of the 10 thoughts in a sequence:

1. My favorite season is the fall. I love the feeling of a cool breeze. (N)
2. I can't wait for summer. I love the feeling of being at camp and going on our annual trip to Florida. (N)
3. I love the pizza at MOD Pizza. It's so delicious. (N)
4. What if that cupcake has dirty germs and makes me sick and I throw up? (OCD)
5. I'm thinking of joining the environmental club at school. (N)
6. I hope to move up to my next belt in tae kwon do this month. (N)
7. I'm wearing neon green socks. (U)
8. I love my brother. We have so much fun playing together. (N)
9. What if I got the stomach flu from sitting next to that girl whose sister had the stomach flu, and now it's on my clothes? (OCD)
10. Drawing is so much fun. I love drawing cities and people. (N)

After the 10 thoughts are written on paper and arranged in order as shown, read the thoughts three times in a row quickly and then say out loud:

"I can see that these are just thoughts. Whether true or not, anxiety-provoking or not, they are just thoughts. Thoughts

are just thoughts, and nothing else. Thoughts have no power unless I give them power."

Practice this once or twice a day, every day, for a few weeks. You can always switch out the OCD thoughts for other OCD thoughts to make the practice better. Remember that the goal is to become an observer of your thoughts, rather than a participant in them. As an observer, you see the thought as just a thought, or just a symptom of OCD. If you participate in the thought, then you will get caught up in what the thought is about (the content of the thought), which makes you stuck in the OCD. Detached mindfulness teaches you how to be aware of and separate from your thoughts, being able to just be an observer of them.

A 13-year-old client of mine practiced this and came in and said, "I think I've got it. Now, when the terrible thoughts come up, I see them as if they are being typed out on a screen in front of me. I cannot really read them or know them, but I see it as just the OCD and it doesn't bother me anymore." This is the goal of detached mindfulness.

Attention Training Technique

Attention training technique (ATT) is also part of metacognitive therapy and was also introduced in Chapter 1. With ATT, the goal is to practice shifting your attention away from worries and obsessive ruminations. It is easy to get caught in the pattern of focusing only on what you are thinking. This technique helps you to break this pattern and become focused on things outside of yourself.

See Dr. Wells's book (see References section for more information), record the 12-minute attention training script, and listen twice a day to learn how to shift your focus and attention away from OCD thoughts. The method involves looking at a dot (I use a red dot) on the wall and keeping your focus on the dot. You also focus on different sounds including a tapping noise, sounds that are occurring naturally around you, and other noises. You learn how to shift your attention between the different sounds. This training process allows you to become skilled at switching your attention away from your worries and obsessive thoughts in your mind and onto other things around you.

Left unchallenged, the OCD will continue to gain power and strength. By continually challenging your OCD, changing what you say to yourself, "stamping" the OCD thoughts, replacing your thoughts, and using detached mindfulness, you will gain power and strength and *take control of OCD!*

What I Know Now

This chapter focused on the thoughts part of OCD. You learned several techniques that focus on learning to see your OCD as separate from yourself: "When my OCD talks, it says . . .", "Stamping" it "OCD," and detached mindfulness. Common OCD thinking patterns were reviewed, and you learned how to replace your anxious thoughts. Finally, self-talk was discussed, and you learned how to have positive self-talk and talk back to your OCD.

6

Challenging Obsessive Thoughts and Worries, PART 2

Loop and Imaginal Exposure Recordings

"When I learned about the idea of making a loop recording and writing down all of my OCD thoughts, I was immediately resistant. The idea of verbalizing these thoughts was so uncomfortable. I was upset about the idea of having this kind of recording on my phone. But once I got over the resistance and understood more about why doing one would help, I just made it and started listening every day. It was hard for the first few days, and then it started to get better. I actually started to hear the thoughts differently and literally became bored by the recording after a few weeks."

—Tyler, age 13

As mentioned in Chapter 5, this chapter will explain the two remaining strategies that you will use to challenge your OCD thoughts. Learning how to make loop recordings is essential, and these plus the ladder are the most important and most effective strategies in overcoming OCD.

When I'm working with clients, we often talk about OCD and anxious thoughts as like cars. Sometimes there are just a few cars on the road, and sometimes there are many and there is a lot of traffic. With OCD, however, the cars usually park themselves in your mind. It's almost like there is a parking lot in your head and the cars that are driving by end up parking there. The goal is to get those cars to keep driving by and to be able to watch them drive by without paying much attention to their size, shape, color, and so forth, and to close your parking lot. Making loop recordings is an excellent way to accomplish this goal.

Another way of conceptualizing your goal when it comes to the OCD thoughts is to imagine that you have two options: Get in a rocky boat, or stay on the steady dock. If you engage in the OCD thoughts and get caught up in them, it's like you are in a rocky boat. However, if you can externalize the OCD thoughts and see them for what they are, you will be able to stay on the steady dock and just look at the boat. Detached mindfulness and loop recordings help in reaching this goal.

Worry Loop and Uncertainty Training Recordings

Worries are thoughts, usually about something bad that might happen, that make you feel anxious. When you have OCD, it becomes particularly difficult to break the cycle of obsessive worrying. This is called "rumination," which refers to the process of getting stuck on thinking about worry thoughts. When you ruminate, you have the same worry thoughts going through your mind over and over, and you find it hard to stop focusing on them. With OCD, it is often hard to see the thoughts as symptoms of OCD. Instead, you just react to the thought and get caught up in it. You end up getting stuck on the *content* of the thought, or what the thought is about, rather than being able to see that the thought is only a symptom of OCD. Once your OCD is triggered and you have these intrusive thoughts in your head, it's hard to disrupt them and you get stuck. One of the main ways to get rid of this symptom is to make a recording of the thoughts, just as they sound in your head, and listen back to that recording over and over, until you habituate, or become bored by, the obsessive thoughts. These recordings are called loop recordings, or worry loop recordings, and have also been called endless loop recordings. I'm sure it sounds like a terrible idea to you to make a recording of your most unwanted, intrusive, and often upsetting thoughts, and then listen back to it over and over again. But doing it this way allows you to break the cycle. No one has ever regretted doing loop recordings. In my practice, I have found that it works wonders for 99% of the kids and teens who do them (I would say 100%, but some people, especially those who have trouble staying focused, have not benefitted as much). The vast majority find it extraordinarily beneficial.

When it comes to not wanting to do the loops, try to remember that you are having these thoughts anyway and this is a way that you can actually challenge them, whereas if you do nothing, they will just continue to happen. Also, by making a recording of these thoughts, it lets you "externalize" them (instead of keeping them to yourself and only in your mind). Although the anxiety will increase for the first few days of listening to the loops, it will go down on day 4 or 5 and then get easier. The practice of listening to your thoughts until they no longer create anxiety for you is the main goal of making a loop recording.

> **worry loop recording:** *a sampling of what your worries sound like (how you hear them) in your mind, made into a recording*

The main reason that loop recordings are so effective is that they capitalize on the biology of the brain. Your brain is programmed to become bored by information that is repeated over and over, or information it already knows. This goes back to cavemen and the goal of finding new land to cover where there could be new berries and new animals to hunt. Our brains are rewarded for finding new information. When the OCD thoughts just happen in your head, they become a habit, and sometimes even feel like new information. When you make those thoughts boring and unalarming, however, the habit can be broken. Think about commercials you've seen over and over—you tune them out—and if you have to hear the same directions being told to you over and over, you tune that out, too. When you make your thoughts into a recording and play it over and over, the brain will become bored by it, and the thoughts will go from alarming to unalarming.

Directions for Making Your Loop

Most kids and teens type or write out their loop before recording it. Another option is to just start the recording. If you have a hard time being able to fluently record your thoughts (for example, if there are many pauses), then I recommend typing it out first.

When recording, just say your thoughts as they sound to you, and try to include the progression of your thoughts. Usually it starts with one thought and then that leads to another and another, and so on. Remind yourself that you want to say *all* of the thoughts you have, even the worst ones, without holding back. Don't leave out thoughts because you are afraid to say them or because you are afraid of the consequences of saying them (these are thinking errors and fusion beliefs, and you need to challenge them by actually saying the thoughts out loud).

Let's go through an example. The following was Alicia's loop recording:

> *What if the milk in my cereal was bad? What if the date was wrong on the carton and it was really expired and I will get sick? What if those cookies were cooked with bad eggs? I will get salmonella and throw up. I will need to wait 48 hours to see if I am okay. I won't know until 48 hours have passed because that's when salmonella comes out. Maybe Mom knows that the milk was expired but is afraid to tell me because I will worry. Mom looked a little worried earlier today. Probably because the milk was expired. Maybe I feel a little sick. Yes, my stomach feels a little nauseous. Oh, no! I'm probably sick with salmonella. I better check the milk again and ask Mom about it and the cookies. Now I will miss school this week and get behind on my work. Like my friend Amber who missed 3 days last week because she was sick. Maybe I got sick from her—I did sit next to her last week at lunch. I might have caught what she caught.*

As you can see, Alicia recorded the loop as her thoughts sounded to her in her mind. Alicia listened to her recording 10 times in a row each day after school. This allowed her to become used to the thoughts themselves. After a few weeks of listening to her recording daily, she habituated to the thoughts, was completely bored by listening to them, and no longer experienced them as alarming. She found that she naturally had less of these automatic thoughts, and when she did, she would recall what she sounded like when she worried, and this caused her to externalize her worries and minimize their strength.

Sometimes, the loops are not stated as "What if . . ." thoughts, but instead are just recordings of the intrusive thoughts. For example, you might remember Ashley, mentioned in Chapter 1, who would get stuck on meaningless parts of math formulas—in particular, what she saw as inconsistencies or flaws in these formulas. Here was her loop:

The math formula is problematic. Those two intersecting lines cannot be equal because the point at which they meet counts as both lines. They cannot be the same. It is not possible to know if the point at which they meet is actually part of both lines. One line might be shorter, but I can't know because the two lines are touching. How can a formula be like this? It doesn't feel like they are the same length. I need to keep thinking about this until it feels right to me. Those lines are not equal. This formula can't be right. That point is double-counted.

For Ashley, just saying these thoughts out loud was an exposure for her, as it could trigger her OCD. Usually, she was afraid to think about a math formula because it would trigger her to get stuck on what she perceived to be a flaw or lack of precision in it. The problem she had with math formulas (her OCD symptom) caused her so much distress that just thinking about it put her at risk for getting triggered into "OCDing" (as she called it), which for her meant that she would think about the formula for *hours* at a time! Thus, she avoided thinking about it and had never talked about it before coming to therapy. Having the thought about the formula itself was her way of challenging the OCD. When Ashley first listened to her recording and heard herself talking about this, she had an immediate change happen: She realized how absurd it was to think this way and how meaningless it was. She heard herself talking and was able to identify her thoughts as OCD. Although most kids don't have this immediate change in perspective, sometimes it happens this way. Whether you do or not, don't worry—just stick with listening to your recording.

Often, the OCD thoughts cause a lot of anxiety for kids, and there can be fears about what it means to even be having these thoughts. For example, one client's OCD focused on thoughts about going crazy and losing his mind. When he would worry about losing his mind, his anxiety level would get so high that he wouldn't be able to concentrate or even speak clearly. Then, he would label his difficulty concentrating and speaking as signs that he was going crazy. For this boy, Derek, his exposure was having the thoughts about going crazy and losing his mind on purpose and getting to the point of not being afraid of having these thoughts. Here is what Derek's loop sounded like:

> *What if I am going crazy? What if I am losing my mind and don't even know it? What will happen to me if I go crazy? Will my family put me somewhere else to live? I can't think and can't speak clearly, so I'm obviously losing my mind. What's wrong with me for having these thoughts? Do all people who go crazy think this way before they lose themselves?*

Like Ashley, Derek's thoughts were so distressing that it took us many weeks to build up to this recording. Then, like everyone who does these recordings, as he listened over and over, not only was he able to tolerate hearing the thoughts, but also his experience of them changed—he was totally bored by and unaffected by these thoughts that had seemed so terrible at first. He was able to see that these thoughts were only symptoms of OCD and anxiety.

The use of recordings is particularly useful for people with OCD who don't do traditional OCD behaviors like checking and washing. For example, Madeline struggled with thoughts of people in her family being harmed and the ways in which they could be hurt. Her OCD included horrible images of what it would look like to hurt someone and how her family would look if they were injured. When making her loop, she talked about her thoughts, the details of what she imagined, and what the images were like. Just talking about the images was an exposure in itself. By doing so, she took a huge step in facing her fears because she had previously tried to avoid these disturbing thoughts and images and had never told anyone about them. Although Madeline didn't do any visible behaviors, she did do mental rituals to avoid her thoughts, including counting the number of items in a room and trying to distract herself with mental lists of what she had to do. When she made her loop recording, she forced herself to be exposed to these disturbing thoughts and images. By listening to the loop repetitively and frequently and for the duration of 30 minutes a day, she was able to habituate to these horrible thoughts and images, so much so that they no longer got to her. With the continual exposures and by facing these images head on (vs. trying to avoid them or resist them), she reduced OCD's power.

Adding Uncertainty Training to Your Loop

The worry loop recording is often a list of many "What if . . ." thoughts. The first part of the recording should be all of the "What if . . ." or whatever intrusive thoughts or worries you experience. The second part will be converting these thoughts into "uncertainty training" thoughts. Basically, you will take your loop, copy and paste it into another paragraph, and then change all of the thoughts in the paragraph to begin with "It's always possible that . . ." or "It's possible that. . . ." Therefore, you will have a longer recording of the same thoughts as they sound in your head and then again as they sound when you make them into "uncertainty training" statements. By doing this, you not only habituate to the thoughts, but also begin to tolerate the uncertainty of if they really happened. OCD is all about uncertainty: It gains power by telling you that you don't know for sure, that it might be, that it could happen. When you translate the thoughts into uncertainty thoughts, you learn how to tolerate the uncertainty and take OCD's power away.

I first learned about uncertainty training from psychologist Dr. Robert Leahy's book *The Worry Cure*, which explained that uncertainty training will help you be better able to tolerate not knowing. Uncertainty training involves saying your fear repeatedly for a practice period every day. It was just like I was doing with all my clients when we made their loops. He explained, for example, that you say: "It is always possible that (add your fear here)" for 10–20 minutes every day. Eventually, you can tolerate the uncertainty of what could happen. When doing this, it is important that you try not to *neutralize* the thought or make it seem less scary. So, you would *not* want to say, "It is always possible that I left the stove on, but most likely I turned it off." That last part—"but most likely I turned it off"—is a neutralizer, and when you add this, you don't get the benefit of really getting used to your fear. Therefore, when you practice, you want to keep your statements to just the worries (do not add ideas that would make you feel better), same as with the regular loop recordings.

For example, Andrew said: "It is always possible that I have germs on my hands from using the bathroom," and "It is always possible that I will get sick." Alicia's statement was: "It is always possible that the milk was expired and I will throw up." Sydney's uncertainty training statement was: "It is always possible that I killed an animal." William said: "It is always possible that I will be punished for having fun and feeling pleasure." Even though these thoughts were very unlikely (if not impossible, for example, in William's case), each person struggled with these thoughts and ideas that these bad outcomes could happen. Their OCD made them believe that the idea was not only possible, but also very likely. Doing the loop with the uncertainty training component allowed them to have a totally different experience of their thoughts, making them neutral and unalarming.

> **uncertainty training:** listening to your thoughts stated as "it's always possible . . ." until you eventually become used to tolerating the uncertainty of what could happen

The following are some examples of worry loops with uncertainty training recordings.

TYLER'S LOOP FOR HIS OCD   EMOTIONAL CONTAMINATION TYPE

Why would that boy kill himself? What could he have been thinking? What if I have the same thoughts? What if I am thinking about what he could have been thinking about and I confuse his thoughts for my own and kill myself also? What if I commit suicide? What if my family never knew that I wasn't really suicidal? What if I died and they thought it was because I really wanted to? What if I'm listening to the Logic song and I hear the lyrics in my head and start believing that those are my thoughts? What if I catch thoughts that I don't want to have from others? What if I don't know my own thoughts from theirs, and what if their opinion becomes mine and I don't know it? What if someone steals my smarts? What if I catch a disability or become an amputee? What if I become disabled? What if I touch the garbage cans and then become a waste collector?

TYLER'S LOOP FOR HIS OCD, continued

It's always possible that I will have the same thoughts as the boy. It is possible that I will think about what he could have been thinking about and end up confusing his thoughts for my own and kill myself also. It's always possible that I will commit suicide. It's possible that my family will never know that I wasn't really suicidal. It's always possible that I would die and they would think it was because I really wanted to. It's always possible that I will listen to the Logic song and hear the lyrics in my head and start believing that those are my thoughts. It's possible that I will catch thoughts that I don't want to have from others. It's always possible that I won't know my own thoughts from theirs. It's possible that their opinion will become mine and I won't know it. It's always possible that someone will steal my smarts. It's possible that I will catch a disability or become an amputee. It's always possible that I will become disabled. It's possible that I will touch the garbage cans and then become a waste collector.

CONNOR'S LOOP FOR HIS OCD   HARM TYPE

What if I hurt someone? What if I do something that will end up hurting someone? What if I get sick and spread it to others because I wasn't careful? What if I knew I could be sick and spread it to others? What if I don't check the oven and stove and Mom's hair dryer and make sure that they are all off and a fire starts and burns down our house? It could have been prevented if I just simply checked. What if I forget to check the doors and windows or decide not to and someone breaks in? What if Mom's phone is low in battery and something happens to her when she's driving? It's my fault if something happens because I didn't check. What if I step on an animal and kill it without even knowing? What if I run over and kill an animal? What if something happens to one of my friends? What if my friends get in an accident because I had them meet me somewhere?

CONNOR'S LOOP FOR HIS OCD, continued

It's always possible that I will hurt someone. It's always possible that I will do something that will end up hurting someone. It's possible that I will get sick and spread it to others because I wasn't careful. It's possible that I knew I could be sick and spread it to others. It's always possible that I won't check the oven and stove and Mom's hair dryer and make sure that they are all off and will then start a fire and burn down our house. It's always possible that I could have prevented it by just simply checking. It's always possible that I will forget to check the doors and windows or decide not to and someone breaks in. It's always possible that Mom's phone battery is low and something happens to her when she's driving. It's possible that it will be my fault if something happens because I didn't check. It's always possible that I stepped on an animal and killed it without even knowing. It's possible that I ran over and killed an animal. It's always possible that something will happen to one of my friends. It's possible that my friends will get in an accident because I had them meet me somewhere.

LINA'S LOOP FOR HER OCD   SEXUAL ORIENTATION TYPE

What if I am a lesbian? What if I'm bisexual? What if I was uncomfortable with Susie changing in front of me because I was actually attracted to her? No other girls seem to get embarrassed. What if I had such a hard time at PE and the pool party because I'm really a lesbian? I didn't see anyone else feeling weird like me. Maybe people who realize that they are gay or lesbian start out just feeling weird. What if I spend time with a lesbian and become one also? What if she kissed me and I kiss her back and found out that I was also lesbian? What if I go out with Sam and realize that I don't have any feelings for him and realize that I'm a lesbian? What if my parents really think I'm a lesbian but they are not telling me because they want me to come out on my own?

LINA'S LOOP FOR HER OCD, continued

It's always possible that I am a lesbian. It's possible that I am bisexual. It's possible that I was uncomfortable with Susie changing in front of me because I was actually attracted to her. It's always possible that no other girls seem to get embarrassed. It's always possible that I had such a hard time at PE and the pool party because I'm really a lesbian. It's possible that no other girls were feeling weird like me. It's always possible that people who realize that they are gay or lesbian start out just feeling weird. It's always possible that I spend time with a lesbian and become one also. It's possible that she might kiss me and I might kiss her back and find out that I am also lesbian. It's always possible that I go out with Sam and realize that I don't have any feelings for him and realize that I'm a lesbian. It's possible that my parents really think I'm a lesbian but they are not telling me because they want me to come out on my own.

Loop Practices and Rationale

Once you've made your loop with uncertainty training, it's time to practice. The goal is to spend 15–20 minutes a day listening to it. If your recording is 2 minutes long, for example, you would listen at least eight times in a row. Remember that the first 4 or 5 days that you listen, your anxiety will go up and you may get triggered by the thoughts. This is normal and part of the process. On day 5 or 6, however, it will get easier to listen to and won't be as triggering. It's a good idea to rate your level of anxiety, from 0 to 10 (with 10 being the highest) each time you practice. This will help you see that you are habituating over time.

You will start to hear the thoughts as OCD symptoms and after 2–4 weeks of practicing every day, you will become bored and habituate to the thoughts. I know this sounds like a lot of time to spend on challenging OCD, but remember that OCD takes time from your life anyway and making this effort will be worth it.

Remember that you are doing this practice to get the thoughts to become boring and unalarming. You are not desensitizing to the *content* of the thought, meaning that you are not trying to be okay with what the thought is saying. The goal is to be able to get bored by hearing the thought, which is just a symptom of OCD. When you focus on the content of the thought—what the thought is about—you end up participating with the thoughts instead of being an observer of them (detached mindfulness). As you do the loop practice, it will become even easier to see your thoughts as just OCD symptoms and not real thoughts deserving of consideration. Also, keep in mind that thoughts have no power unless you give them power.

Another key point is that when you are listening to the uncertainty training part, the goal is to be able to feel the emotions that accompany these thoughts and the uncertainty. It's like building a muscle for being able to tolerate uncertainty. The more you practice, the stronger your muscle will become.

Most kids and teens will end up making several loops. Often, you will think of new OCD thoughts while listening to your first loop and will end up making a second one. Then, as you are working through the OCD, you will find other themes that should become loops. It's not uncommon for someone who is working through OCD to end up making 5–10 different loops. It's also a strategy that you can use down the road if, once you've overcome OCD, it comes back at all. In this case, you can use loop recordings again.

Although the majority of people reading this book will make a worry loop, some will not. It is up to you to decide if it fits your type of OCD symptoms. For example, some OCD is just compulsions without thoughts or worries, and in this case, the treatment will be mostly about doing the exposure work (ERP). One final note is about the "need to confess" type of OCD: For those with this type, sometimes the loops can become a compulsion in that making a loop is another way of "confessing." In this case, I like to limit the number of loops to five or fewer.

Imaginal Exposure Recordings

Another very useful strategy in treating OCD is making an imaginal exposure recording. This is when you make a story about your worst OCD fears playing out. It is either written or recorded (or both). Even though this is a form of exposure, I've included it in this chapter because I will be recommending that you make it into a recording, and because it is one of the best ways to challenge your OCD thoughts. I typically only use imaginal exposures with older teens, like those who are 15–18 years old, and with adults, as they can be pretty challenging to listen to. In general, loop recordings are enough for most people with OCD. There are certain times when I have used it with younger children. For example, as you will see later in this section, Tyler and Lina both used and benefitted from this technique. If you read the following description and feel that imaginal exposure recordings could be useful for you, then I recommend you make one.

Imaginal exposure recordings are narratives of your feared OCD thoughts and images and what could happen if those situations actually happened. This technique really helps you to learn to tolerate uncertainty as well because you are playing out what could happen. The recordings are imaginal exposure to what *could* happen. Like the loop recordings, they will initially cause your anxiety to go up, but also like loop recordings, the anxiety will go down as you continue to listen over and over. Often, there is resistance to doing this strategy (like loops), as they are scary at first. It's important to remind yourself (and I know I keep repeating this) that thoughts have no power unless you give them power. Just thinking about something does not mean that it is true or that it will happen. Just thinking about your worst fears playing out does not mean it will happen. Remember that this is how OCD gains its power: It thrives on what "could" or what "might" happen—it thrives on uncertainty. Therefore, by tolerating uncertainty and habituating to the thoughts from listening to loops and imaginal exposure recordings, you are taking OCD's power away.

Directions for Making Your Imaginal Exposure Recording

The goal in making imaginal exposure recordings is to write out exactly the feared situation as it could play out. You want to make it into a narrative and record it as you did with the loops from the first person "I . . ." perspective, or as it sounds in your mind. Come up with a feared scenario and write down the following:

> all of your anxious or scary thoughts,
> what you are worried about happening,
> how you feel and any physical sensations of anxiety or fear,
> any compulsion you want to do, and

> the worst thing that could happen if this situation did happen (try to push it to the furthest "What if . . . ?" and "What if that happened?" and "Then if that happened, what would happen next?").

Once you have written these notes, make them into a narrative, sort of like you are telling a story but as if the story is happening to you. Write everything from first person "I." You might need to make the recording a few times to make sure to include all of the thoughts and feelings that would make it seem real.

The goal is to make multiple imaginal exposure recordings, but even doing just one will be useful. As you will see in the following examples, the imaginal exposure recordings can seem very intense and scary. It may help, if you are younger and reading this book, to read this section with a parent, just so you can talk about it after and process if it is a technique that you should use. It's essential to include this in the book to show how imaginal exposure recordings work for these scary OCD thoughts and images. The imaginal exposure recordings reflect one's most feared scenarios. Keep in mind that these clients all had these scenarios play out in their minds, and the scenarios made them feel very anxious and stressed and made the OCD stronger. By making their scenarios into recordings and listening to them over and over, they were able to become free from the thoughts and images.

The following are examples of imaginal exposure recordings for Tyler, Connor, and Lina.

TYLER'S IMAGINAL EXPOSURE FOR HIS OCD
EMOTIONAL CONTAMINATION TYPE

I'm sitting in my room reading for English class. Mom is downstairs making dinner and Dad is out walking the dog. It's about 6 p.m. and I remember that boy killed himself around this time of day. I start thinking about that boy and how he committed suicide. His life ended, and he is over. Why would he do that? What was he thinking? What thoughts could he have had to make him kill himself? Did he think it would never get better? What about his parents? Mom would never be okay if I died. Neither would Dad.

TYLER'S IMAGINAL EXPOSURE FOR HIS OCD, continued

Their hearts would be broken, and they would never be the same. I can't imagine what he was thinking. I come up with an idea of what he was thinking. Then I can't tell if they are his thoughts or my thoughts. I start to think they are my thoughts. Yes, these are my thoughts. They must be because I am thinking them. I am thinking them just like the boy did. I decide that I will jump off a bridge just like he did. I then leave the house and drive to the nearest bridge and jump off. I die instantly. My life ends in that moment. I never go to college, never become an adult. My parents find out and can't believe I committed suicide. My mom is crying uncontrollably. My father is holding her and crying also. They never know that I wasn't really suicidal. Their lives are ruined. Then they have a funeral for me. I can see everyone there and they are all crying.

CONNOR'S IMAGINAL EXPOSURE FOR HIS OCD   HARM TYPE

I am out to lunch with friends and sitting next to Jack who seems to have a cold. He sneezes and it gets on me. I leave lunch and can't stop thinking that I am sick. A few days later, Jack texts me that he has the flu. I then realize I have the flu and gave it to my grandparents who I saw yesterday. I call my grandpa and he doesn't answer. I decide to go over there. Grandpa is lying in bed, coughing and having trouble breathing. He is so sick and clearly has the flu. My grandma is lying on the couch, also with the flu. How could I have been so irresponsible? What if they die because of my recklessness? How could I have been so careless?

LINA'S IMAGINAL EXPOSURE FOR HER OCD
SEXUAL ORIENTATION TYPE

Susie comes over for a sleepover. I haven't seen her in a while and am very excited. Almost too excited. I know that it's not normal to be so excited to see your best friend. I think I like her. Yes, I must like her because I am getting too excited. Then she comes over and we order pizza. I let her pick the toppings, just like someone would let their girlfriend choose. I look at her, and wow, she is pretty. I've never noticed how pretty she is. We are sitting next to each other on the couch, and I inch closer until our arms touch. I then lean my head on her shoulder, pretending to be tired. I'm doing this only because I want to touch her. She doesn't know this, but she doesn't do anything. My heart is beating fast and I have butterflies in my stomach. Then I start to touch her hair and realize I am definitely a lesbian. Before bed, we are changing into our pajamas and I watch her as she changes. I am looking at her without her shirt on, and yes, I am a lesbian.

The next day I have lunch with the girl who came out as lesbian. She asked me out, and I said yes. At lunch, she leans over and rests her head on my shoulder. I get a thrill from this and now know for sure that I am a lesbian. She starts to kiss me and I don't resist. In fact, I like it. My heart is beating fast and I have those butterflies again. I'm definitely lesbian, I know for sure, and now I tell my parents. They reassure me that it's okay, and actually, they knew all along that I was gay. Deep down, I know I have disappointed them.

Tyler, Connor, and Lina all found it very hard to make their narratives. I helped them make the imaginal exposure recordings as detailed as possible. For the first week, listening to the imaginal exposure recordings was very hard, and very anxiety-provoking. It started to get easier in the second week and then even easier after that, eventually leading to habituation. Doing these recordings also made it clearer to each of them what the OCD sounded like and how overexaggerated the thoughts and images could be.

Imaginal Exposure Practices and Rationale

The practice for imaginal exposure recordings is essentially the same as for loops. You want to listen to the entire recording during a prolonged period once a day. Most imaginal exposure recordings are at least 10 minutes long. Regardless of the length of the recording, you want to listen for at least 20–30 minutes each day. If you can do it longer, that's great. The longer, the better. I know it sounds very time-consuming, but keep in mind that OCD itself is time-consuming. At least when you are doing imaginal exposure recordings, the time you spend dealing with OCD is time spent challenging and overcoming it. As it will be too time-consuming for most kids and teens to do both loop and imaginal exposure recordings at the same time, I recommend doing loops for 3–4 weeks and then imaginal exposure recordings for the following 3–4 weeks.

Again, the goal with imaginal exposure practices is to become used to, or habituate to, the fearful scenarios that make the OCD so strong. By doing this, you will be better able to handle the uncertainty of these situations, and this will make them less powerful.

What I Know Now

This chapter focused on teaching you how to make loop with uncertainty training recordings and imaginal exposure recordings. You learned that by listening to your OCD thoughts, including putting them in uncertainty format, and by listening to feared scenarios play out as a recorded story, you can habituate to the thoughts, tolerate uncertainty, and take OCD's power away. You also learned that you will be better able to see the thoughts as just OCD thoughts, which supports detached mindfulness. We discussed thoughts as being like cars that drive by, instead of parking in your mind, and staying on the steady dock instead of getting in the rocky boat. Finally, the idea that you are not becoming "okay" with the content of the thought, but simply getting bored by hearing the thought itself, is the goal in this practice.

Tolerating Uncertainty

"The hardest part of having OCD is that the worry doesn't end. I worry about how something may have happened that will cause me to be sick years from now. It's about the uncertainty of what will happen. Maybe I won't know that I got contaminated with some illness that won't come out until much later."

—Frank, age 13

One of the main difficulties faced by children with OCD is being able to tolerate uncertainty. Uncertainty means not knowing for sure. Tolerating something means being able to handle it. So, being able to *tolerate uncertainty* means being able to handle not knowing for sure. In the last chapter, you did uncertainty training as part of the loop recordings. This chapter focuses a little more on dealing with uncertainty in general.

When you have OCD, it makes you feel like you need to know for absolute sure that something did or didn't happen, or that something could or could not happen. OCD causes you to keep repeating the thoughts of "What if . . . ?" and worrying about what might have happened. This desire for certainty is at the root of many of your OCD worries, thoughts, and behaviors, particularly the urge to check and recheck over and over. The goal is to challenge those thoughts and learn how to be okay with not knowing.

> **tolerating uncertainty:** being able to handle not knowing for sure

OCD and Uncertainty

As you work toward taking control of OCD, you are figuring out how OCD influences your thinking and twists the way that you see things. You are starting to see how OCD works and how it makes you think. For example, OCD makes you focus on potential threats. It keeps your attention focused on what could go wrong. OCD also gets stronger and more powerful when there is uncertainty, or ambiguity, in a situation. When something is ambiguous, it is unclear, vague, or uncertain. If there is any room for doubt, OCD will try to gain power from it. As discussed in Chapter 5, this desire for certainty is a type of OCD thinking pattern.

The ironic thing about OCD is that it tells you that you can't have doubts, but creates doubt all of the time. When there is doubt, it makes you want to check or get reassurance, and doing so only makes the OCD stronger. This is how OCD makes you feel trapped in your thoughts and behaviors.

For example, when Sydney stepped on something without seeing what it was, the OCD would make her worry that it was an animal that she stepped on. Because she didn't see what she stepped on, there was some uncertainty in the situation. Even though she would have known if she had stepped on an animal, the OCD made her think that she could've stepped on an animal without knowing it. The OCD made her doubt what happened.

This idea of not knowing what you did, or what you saw, is a big theme in OCD. I have worked with many children and teens who have worried that they did something, such as leave the oven on, leave the door open or unlocked, or hurt someone, and many of them worry that they did these things without knowing it or without remembering it. In this way, OCD can make you doubt what you know. It is very important that you recognize that this type of thinking and this type of experience are only *symptoms* of OCD.

Doubts: Where Checking Behavior Comes From

Checking is a common OCD behavior (ritual), usually done to decrease the anxiety that comes from an upsetting thought about something bad happening. Therefore, checking comes from doubts about what might have occurred. When there is any amount of uncertainty, OCD makes you doubt. Because Sydney had doubts about what she stepped on, she retraced her steps to make sure she hadn't hurt any animals. Alicia had doubts about the safety of the food she ate, so she would check the expiration dates again, or would ask her mom to tell her she was safe. Asking her mom was another form of checking behavior ("I am checking with Mom to make sure the food was safe"). Connor would retrace his steps and drive back over his route again to make sure he didn't hurt anything. Sometimes Kevin would get so worried and anxious that he might have hurt a younger child without knowing it that he would check the newspaper to make sure there were no reports that he had done so.

The motivation for these checking behaviors is to try to know something for sure. The motivation is certainty. The problem is that OCD makes you feel like you could *never* be certain. Even when you check and try to know something for sure, OCD will not be satisfied—OCD will still make you have doubts and want you to keep checking, over and over again. The only solution is to learn how to tolerate uncertainty, hang out with it, and not respond with any actions.

Uncertainty as a Part of Life

As much as we would like to know how things will turn out, this is not how life goes. And, to be honest with you, life would not be that enjoyable or exciting if we were able to know how things will turn out. Part of the joy of life is watching it unfold and experiencing things that come along in your life when they naturally come along. Part of overcoming OCD is talking back to it and telling it that you won't try to gain certainty, not only because you don't want to be ruled by OCD, but also because gaining certainty is not possible. We all live with risk, much of the time not even thinking about most risks that exist. OCD focuses on certain risks, and no amount of logic or reasoning will ever make you feel certain or without risk. The goal is to accept it and not let OCD control your behaviors by causing you to try to find certainty.

As you grow up, one life goal is to work toward accepting that uncertainty is a part of life, and to try your hardest (using the strategies described in this book) to enjoy life without worrying so much about it. You can use mindfulness and practice being in the present moment to help you reach the goal of accepting uncertainty.

The loops and imaginal exposure recordings will help you be able to deal with the uncertainty and fears that OCD creates. These techniques help you tolerate your scariest thoughts. Most OCD thoughts are about doubts: Was I careful enough? Did I check that was unplugged? Would I hurt someone? Is it safe for me to be around other children? Will I get sick? Is this a symptom of a terminal illness? The thoughts are typically rooted in doubt and uncertainty, which creates anxiety or discomfort, and then in efforts to reduce this anxiety, you do compulsions and rituals. Yet, the compulsions and rituals only work for a short amount of time. Once you have the thoughts again, you start from scratch and have the same desire for certainty (that's why there is an OCD cycle). The exposure practice (ERP) also helps you tolerate uncertainty, as by facing your fears and avoiding compulsions, you are essentially practicing uncertainty. For example, when Connor practiced driving down the road without retracing his route, he was practicing tolerating uncertainty.

He learned to be okay with these doubts, and by practicing over and over, he eventually stopped doubting altogether. Finally, psychologist Dr. Jonathan Abramowitz, another OCD expert, talked about "lifestyle exposure," which can also be called "exposure lifestyle" and referred to the idea that you need to embrace exposures and make them a part of your daily life. Instead of just doing practices and trying one step from your ladder a day, make the practice broader and take every opportunity you can to practice facing your fears and facing the OCD. By doing this, you will be better able to tolerate uncertainty.

When you worry, you associate not knowing with danger, but not knowing is actually neither good nor bad—it is just neutral. This is similar to when you challenge thinking errors by replacing the negative thoughts with neutral ones. It's the same concept: When you don't know something for sure, try to make it something neutral, rather than something bad. So, you might say to yourself, "Not knowing for sure is neither good nor bad. It is in between. The outcome can be good or bad, but at this moment in time, it is simply neutral."

Tolerating Uncertainty Versus Self-Talk

It is important to make clear the difference between when to tolerate uncertainty and when to reduce the anxiety and reassure yourself by using self-talk. It's easy to see that these are two opposite, or contradictory, techniques. Self-talk involves telling yourself that it will be okay, that you are scared but safe, while tolerating the uncertainty focuses on being able to handle the idea of not knowing if you are safe or if things will turn out okay. These two can, and should, be used to take control of OCD, but the difference is *when* you use each:

> **Self-talk** is good to use when you are actually doing the exposures and facing your fears, especially in the beginning. It's also best to use self-talk when you are really activated and having a hard time with the OCD. It helps you manage the challenge of facing your fears and prevents your rituals. It helps you to be stronger and gain more confidence in taking control of OCD.

> **Tolerating uncertainty**, on the other hand, is not usually beneficial in the beginning of doing the exposures or facing your fears. Instead, start with uncertainty training as a separate prac-

tice that you do at a different time, preferably as part of your loop recordings. The uncertainty training will help you be better able to manage doubts and not knowing for sure and will ultimately help you manage the exposures better. Once you have been able to do a step on your ladder with ease, then you can add in the uncertainty training statements, such as "It's possible that . . . I am sick and spreading it to others" while you are doing the exposure. Once you get to that point, you are doing the hardest and most effective ERP, as you are challenging the thoughts and the behavior at the same time.

What I Know Now

This chapter focused on helping you learn how to be able to handle uncertainty and discussed the connection between OCD and a desire for certainty. The connection between doubts and checking behavior also was explained. You learned that uncertainty is a part of life, and that being able to accept this is part of growing up. Finally, you learned about the difference between when to use self-talk and when to practice tolerating uncertainty.

8

OCD and Other Conditions

"Working through my OCD was extra hard because of my ADHD. I found it hard to pay attention to the loop recordings, so we had to come up with a different way of doing them. I also have perfectionism, so I had to work on that when doing the exposures. My OCD likes everything to be straight and in a line, and it came up a lot in my schoolwork. I learned how to deal with all of these and gradually got rid of the OCD."

—Luke, age 15

It is very common for children with OCD to have another anxiety disorder and/or a mood disorder. When this happens, it's called a "comorbidity." About 50%–90% of children and teens with OCD have another psychological disorder, most commonly another anxiety disorder, ADHD, or a mood disorder, such as depression. The goal is to treat the other disorder in addition to treating the OCD. Usually when the OCD improves, the other anxiety or mood disorder will improve as well. It is important to know that the other disorder does impact the treatment process and might need to be addressed as well. The other disorder also may influence the kind of medications you may take. For example, stimulant medications prescribed for ADHD sometimes make OCD symptoms worse and cause anxiety. Other times, the stimulants make the ADHD better so the anxiety goes down. It's different for different people.

> **comorbidity:** when you have two disorders at the same time; if you have OCD and another anxiety disorder, that second anxiety disorder is called a comorbid disorder

The following is a list of other common problems or conditions that may co-occur with OCD:

> > **Generalized anxiety:** Chronic worrying that lasts for at least 6 months, usually about a lot of different things, accompanied by feeling restless, having muscle tension, and finding it hard to concentrate.
> > **Separation anxiety:** Having a very hard time separating from your parent(s), or the main caregiver, and worrying something could happen to them (or to you). Often, kids with separation anxiety have trouble sleeping alone or going to bed on their own.
> > **Social anxiety:** Worrying about being judged negatively by others, which makes it hard to join new groups, express your preferences, raise your hand in class, and perform in front of others.
> > **Panic attacks:** Having a very strong feeling of fear that causes a lot of physical anxiety, including rapid heartbeat or heart palpitations, difficulty breathing or feelings of choking, dizziness/lightheadedness, trembling/shaking, tingling or numbness in your hands or feet, fear of dying, fear of going crazy, and feeling like you are not in your body. Panic attacks come on and peak, then start to decrease.

> **Specific phobia:** Being very scared of something, such as dogs, flying on an airplane, or getting a shot. You either avoid the thing you are terrified of, or you get extremely distressed while near it.

> **Attention Deficit/Hyperactivity Disorder (ADHD):** This involves having trouble staying focused or being easily distracted, losing things, impulsivity (doing things without thinking it through first), constantly feeling like you need to move, and having trouble sitting still. These symptoms can make schoolwork very challenging, and it can also cause problems in one's social life. Many kids with ADHD take medication for it, which usually helps a great deal.

> **Tic disorders:** Tics are either motor (movement) or verbal. When you have motor tics, you feel the urge to move a part of body (twitching, rolling your head or neck, blinking eyes, straightening your arm). Verbal tics could involve repetitive throat clearing or making certain sounds. Tics are very common, especially in boys, and often are experienced as annoying.

> **Tourette syndrome:** This is a more significant version of a tic disorder, where you have two or more motor tics *and* at least one verbal tic. These tics are chronic and last for a year or more.

> **Body dysmorphic disorder:** This is when a person is preoccupied with a part of their body that seems flawed or defective. The person has a distorted view of a part of their body, and often the flaw is minor, nonexistent, or unnoticeable to others. For example, it could be a mark on the face or a part of one's arm that appears as defective to the individual. Body dysmorphic disorder is beyond just negative body image, and it involves an obsessiveness with part(s) of the body.

> **Trichotillomania:** This is often referred to as "hair-pulling disorder" or "trich" and involves the continual pulling of hair on the body. Most often, it's hair from the head but can also be eyebrows or eyelashes.

> **Excoriation:** This term is used to describe chronic skin-picking that often results in bleeding, scarring, or sores.

> **Hoarding:** This is when someone collects and saves an enormous amount of stuff and refuses to get rid of it. The amount of stuff is usually so large that it causes a problem for the person. Hoarding is more than just having a messy room or finding it hard to get rid of things like toys or old books. Rather, hoarding is a more serious problem in which the person's possessions get

in the way of normal activity, such as when a room is so full of stuff that it can't be used for other purposes or there is so much in one space that it is a fire hazard.

> **Perfectionism:** When you have unrealistically high standards that can most likely never be met. Perfectionists are harsh and judging with themselves, often have low self-esteem, and are usually dissatisfied with their performance or that of others.

> **Health anxiety:** This is when you are preoccupied with having a serious illness and the worry continues even after you see a doctor. Usually this involves repeated checking, scanning for symptoms, seeking reassurance, and seeking medical opinions.

One of the key defining characteristics of all of these issues is that they cause an interference in daily life, and they usually cause distress for the person. Each of these issues should be treated in addition to the OCD. As I noted, often the OCD treatment will help with these issues, but it needs to be directly integrated into the OCD treatment.

Depression is one of the most commonly co-occurring conditions with OCD. Sometimes, the OCD comes on first, and when it doesn't go away or get treated, it can result in depression. Sometimes, depression comes first and then OCD appears later. Depression is when you feel sad for most days of the week and find it hard to break away from the sadness or to feel better. Depression often makes you feel less interested in activities that you used to enjoy. Children with depression may cry or tear up easily, feel bad about themselves or feel guilty, feel tired or have low energy, have trouble sleeping or sleep too much, not eat enough or overeat, and especially in boys, be very irritable or agitated. Usually, children with depression just feel this way, maybe out of the blue, rather than having an event cause them to be depressed. When there is an event that happens that causes a child to feel very sad or depressed, such as when a best friend moves away or when parents get divorced, this is *not* called a depressive disorder. Instead, it is a normal reaction to an upsetting event. Depression can be serious and can sometimes make children think about death or about killing themselves. If this happens to you, you should talk to your parents, or to another caring adult, and get professional help immediately. With treatment, depression will improve.

When ADHD occurs with OCD, the loop recordings may be hard to listen to. In this case, I will usually have the loop typed out and have the child or teen read the loop out loud over and over, until habituation occurs. Also, it can be helpful to do the loop practices during times of the day when focus is better, either just after waking, or if on medication, during medicated periods. The goal is to not get frustrated with yourself for having trouble focusing when listening to the loop, and rather problem solve to make the techniques work better for you.

For health anxiety, I recommend completing a daily health symptom log. This is something you can record in a notebook by making five columns and labeling them as follows: date, symptom you worried about, disease or illness you worried about, level of anxiety (1–10), and any checking or reassurance behavior you did. Take a look at the "Daily Health Log" graphic as an example.

Daily Health Log

Date	Symptom I Worried About	Disease or Illness I Worried About	Level of Anxiety (1–10)	Checking or Reassurance Behavior I Did

When it comes to trichotillomania and skin-picking, it's best to use a self-monitoring form to keep track of when you pick. Doing this really decreases the amount of picking. For this and many other specific disorders, there are books listed in the Resources section at the back of this book.

What I Know Now

This chapter focused on helping you learn about other problems that may occur along with OCD and offered some tips on how to deal with some of them. If you experience depression, make sure to report it to your parent(s) or school counselor, and remember that therapy is very effective, especially CBT, in treating depression. For ADHD, the goal is to be patient and problem solve to make loops more effective. For health anxiety and picking/pulling disorders, keeping a log and self-monitoring is very useful.

9

Facing Your Fears

Exposure/Response Prevention

"Even though it's hard to deal with, eventually you get through it. If you work toward it and concentrate, in the end it's worth it—it gets easier."

—Sophie, age 12

Congratulations on getting to this chapter! Up until now, all of the chapters have been focused on helping you get to this point. By learning about OCD, challenging your thoughts, and preparing for the phase of challenging your OCD behaviors, you are now ready to start facing your fears! This chapter and the next one are about doing exposures, which address the *behavior* part of OCD.

Before we get into it, let's review everything you have learned up until this point:

> Definition of OCD
> Common types of obsessions and compulsions
> OCD thinking patterns and beliefs (such as overrating danger, desire for certainty)
> The OCD cycle
> Cognitive-behavioral therapy (CBT; the most effective treatment for OCD)
> The three parts of OCD/anxiety: body, thoughts, and behavior
> Relaxation techniques, including:
>> Calm breathing (lower diaphragmatic breathing and one-nostril breathing)
>> Progressive muscle relaxation (PMR)
>> Relaxing imagery
>> Mindfulness meditation
>> Yoga

> Medication
> Being proactive and hopeful and asking for support
> How to identify your OCD thoughts ("When my OCD talks, it says . . .")
> "Stamping" it "OCD"
> Positive self-talk
> Distraction
> Thinking mistakes (for example, catastrophizing, superstitious thinking, shoulds, fusion beliefs)
> How to replace your anxious thoughts
> Metacognitive therapy (MCT; including detached mindfulness and attention training technique)
> Using loop recordings with uncertainty training
> Using imaginal exposure recordings
> Tolerating uncertainty
> Exposure/response prevention (ERP)

> The importance of making a ladder and how to make your own
> Sample ladders of children and teens with OCD

If any part of this list seems unfamiliar or like you may have forgotten it, then it is a good idea to go back and review the sections in the previous chapters, as all of the information is useful and important for facing your fears.

Exposure/Response Prevention (ERP)

In Chapter 2, you learned about the idea of "exposure" to your feared situations and that exposure/response prevention (ERP) is the best way to overcome OCD. You've reviewed many sample ladders showing how the exposure practices are structured. As explained before, ERP involves facing your fears, one by one, and preventing yourself from doing the ritual or behavior that you usually do in response to that situation. For example, Andrew would sit next to someone who was sick (exposure) without washing his hands afterward (response prevention). Alicia would eat food from bake sales and sample trays in grocery stores (exposures) without asking questions afterward, such as asking the people at the bake sale about their cooking methods and asking her mom to assure her that she would not get sick (response preventions). Jasmine would mismatch her socks in her closet (exposure) without rearranging them to make them "correct" (response prevention), and she would turn things around in her room (exposure) without adjusting them back to their "correct" positions (response prevention). Kevin would walk by parks with children playing to purposefully have the OCD thoughts about hurting them (exposure), without shaking his head (response prevention). When you do ERP, you challenge the OCD and train yourself to respond appropriately, as someone without OCD would.

When Andrew, Alicia, Jasmine, Connor, Tyler, Lina, and Kevin did their exposures, their anxiety levels increased at first: They felt anxious and had many anxious thoughts. Without doing their usual "neutralizing rituals" or behaviors that they would do to decrease their anxiety, they would feel more of the anxiety. Each of these children and teens had to remind themselves that it would get worse before it got better and that they would have anxiety in the short-term (when doing ERP) in order to be anxiety-free in the long-term. They had to remember that although their usual rituals and behaviors helped them to feel relief in the moment, those rituals and behaviors actually strengthened their OCD and kept OCD around in the future. They reminded themselves that it was them versus the OCD. Andrew, Alicia, Jasmine, Connor, Tyler, Lina, and Kevin also used all of the strategies they learned to be able to cope with the exposures. For example, they used calm breathing, positive self-talk, and replacement thoughts to be better able to handle the exposures.

In addition to becoming used to the practices and learning that nothing bad happens, the goal is also to be able to tolerate the emotions that come up when you are facing your fears. Remember that distraction techniques should *not* be used when you are doing ERP because they take the attention away from the exposures and the feelings that come up. The goal is to be 100% mindful during the exposures, so you can get the most from practicing. Distraction *can* be used, however, after the exposure practices to prevent rumination.

Why Exposure Works

The theory behind exposure is that once you stay in a scary or uncomfortable situation long enough and practice it enough times, you will get used to it, and it will no longer cause you to feel anxious. As you've already learned, this process is called "habituation," which means that you will habituate to, or get used to, the situation. Just as you have learned to habituate to the OCD thoughts, you will learn to habituate to the exposure situations. Remember that the brain is designed to become bored by information that it already knows. When you practice the ladder situations, the same thing will happen.

> **habituation:** once you stay in a scary or uncomfortable situation long enough and practice it enough times, you will get used to it, and it will no longer cause you to feel anxious

The best way to understand habituation is to think about a freezing cold swimming pool. If you were to jump in and then jump out immediately, you would conclude that pools are unpleasant and uncomfortable. If you continued to do this (quickly jumping in and out) each time you saw a freezing cold swimming pool, all you would do is strengthen this belief that pools are uncomfortable and that you don't like them. However, if you got in the pool and made yourself stay there, you would gradually become more relaxed and more comfortable, and you would learn that pools are not that bad after all. After 5 minutes, you would start to breathe easier, then after 10 minutes, you would be able to go farther in, and after 15 minutes, you would no longer feel freezing. In fact, the water would start to feel warmer to you—even though the water temperature itself didn't really change (for example, anyone new to come into the pool would consider it freezing)—because you have become used to it. The longer you stayed in it, the more comfortable you would feel. It's the same thing with anxiety and OCD: Once you stay in an anxiety-provoking situation for long enough, it will no longer cause you to feel anxiety. Your anxiety will decrease, and the situation itself will become more neutral to you.

When you do the exposures and take the steps on your ladder, you will see the process of habituation happen. You will see yourself becoming more comfortable in situations you have typically avoided in the past.

When you challenge your OCD purposefully by doing the exposures on your ladder, you shift the power so that OCD has less power and you have more. This change in the power dynamic allows you to take control of OCD. By being in your trigger situations without doing the behaviors you usually do (such as repetitive checking), you have the chance to learn that your beliefs about bad things happening are untrue. You also become one step closer to not being organized or influenced by OCD because you will be able to prevent yourself from doing the OCD behaviors.

Three Keys to Doing Exposures

When doing exposures, you want to keep in mind the three keys to exposure:
1. repetitive,
2. frequent, and
3. prolonged.

You want to do each step on your ladder *repetitively*, meaning that you do that step over and over again until it no longer causes you anxiety. Once you have practiced a step enough times for it to not cause you anxiety, then it should be part of your normal behavior. Therefore, you repeat each step many times until it no longer belongs on your ladder!

You want to do the exposure to the step *frequently*, meaning that you practice taking the step as often as possible. When you do something frequently, you do it a lot. So, in addition to practicing the same step over and over (compared to just doing it once), you practice that step often and many times (frequently). Ideally, you should plan to do practices from your ladder almost every day (because most kids with OCD do their OCD behaviors every day).

You want to stay in the exposure for a *prolonged* period of time, long enough to see your anxiety level decrease. Prolonged means for a long, extended period of time. If you only stay in the situation for a short time, it will be harder to get used to it. Also, if you do this, you may reinforce, or strengthen, your negative feelings about the situation. Because you didn't stay in it long enough to reach the point of calming down, then you will only remember that you felt anxious. Think about the swimming pool again: If you didn't like pools in the first place, and then quickly jumped in and out, all you would do would be to reinforce or strengthen your belief that swimming pools are uncomfortable. You would only remember how freezing cold it was and how cold you were, and you would not have had the chance to get used to it and realize that it would feel warm in about 15 minutes!

> **prolonged:** for a long, extended period of time; you want to stay in the exposure long enough to see your anxiety level decrease

So, when you do the steps on your ladder, make sure to **repeat** each step, do it **frequently**, and stay in it for a **prolonged** period of time!

Finally, you want to engage your parents and/or siblings or friends in helping you with your ladder practices. Ask your parents to help you create your exposures and ensure that they don't reassure you or accommodate the OCD. Most families accommodate the OCD, and we want your family to discontinue this, as it only makes the OCD stronger. When you show your ladder items to them, explain what they need to do, or not do, to help you make the practices robust.

Using Your Ladder and Planning Your Exposures

In Chapter 3, you developed your ladder and ranked the situations that make you anxious that you tend to avoid. Now is the time to refer to your ladder and plan your first exposure.

Your ladder will guide you on what steps to take and the order in which you should take them. As a general rule, you should take one step at a time and not move ahead to the next step until you have habituated to the step below it. Again, you may realize along the way that the order you put your steps in might need to be changed. It also is very important to remember that you can break steps down into smaller steps. The main goal is to be working on your exposures, even if you are breaking them down into very small steps. We care more about progression than pace, meaning that as long as you're practicing and moving forward, you don't need to worry about how quickly you are doing it.

Start with making a plan to take the first step on the ladder, including which coping strategies you will use. The more detailed your plan, the better. For example, Jasmine's first step was to leave her backpack zipper partially opened. She developed the following plan to take the step, including which strategies would help:

> *Unzip my backpack and then when zipping it back up, leave a gap of about 2 inches. Immediately take a step back from the backpack (so it's not within my arm's reach) and do calm breathing to stay as relaxed as possible. While looking at the zipper and noticing how it's not zipped correctly, use self-talk to remind myself that I need to stay with the feelings of discomfort and that I will feel better soon. Also, remind myself that this wouldn't bother most people and it's only bothering me because of OCD. I can't listen to the OCD anymore. I will get to the point where I realize that it doesn't matter that the zipper is not fully closed and that I can feel okay even when I don't fix it.*

Thinking about how she will handle her feelings of discomfort and identifying specific strategies that she will use (calm breathing, self-talk),

Jasmine was able to be successful during the exposure and prevent her usual response of zipping the backpack completely.

Jasmine continued to make detailed plans for the first several steps. For example, her third step was to pack an odd number of underwear, shorts, and T-shirts for sleepaway camp. She developed the following plan to take the step, including which strategies would help:

> *Plan to pack on Sunday and have Mom help me with what to bring. Because I am packing for 2 weeks and will get to wash my clothes, I will pack nine pairs of underwear, five pairs of shorts, and seven T-shirts. As soon as I've picked out the clothes, I will have Mom put them in the duffel bag and move the duffel bag to the garage. This way, I won't be tempted to add anything to it. I will use calm breathing if I notice my body feeling tense and self-talk to remind myself that I can handle this and that it will be okay. I also will remind myself that I am practicing being able to let things be, even though it doesn't feel right to me. I believe that if I stick with it, the urge to add more clothes to make an even number will go away. If I continue to focus on it, I will try distraction by repeating the ABCs and making lists, or I will use detached mindfulness to separate myself from my thoughts and try to become an observer to my thoughts, rather than reacting to them.*

After developing plans for the first several steps, Jasmine got the hang of it and didn't need to do as much preparation for the rest of the steps. Throughout the exposure period, however, she continued to review her self-talk statements and kept a journal of her thoughts, labeling her thinking errors and OCD beliefs as they came up.

Similarly, William made detailed plans for many of the steps on his ladder, which included the strategies he would use to cope with anxiety during the exposures. His first step was to not do homework on weekend nights. He ranked this step the easiest because there had been weekend nights in the past when he did not do homework and felt fine, but these were the exception to the rule, as he usually did homework on Friday and Saturday evenings.

William planned to rent a movie on Friday night and planned to go out with his friends on Saturday night. We discussed that going out with his friends was going to be harder because it was more fun, and he felt guilty when he was having fun and enjoying himself. He planned to watch the movie in the basement, away from his desk and homework, and to use self-talk to deal with any anxiety or discomfort that came up. He made the following self-talk note cards for this situation: "It is perfectly reasonable to watch a movie and relax on a weekend night. I have worked hard all week and need this downtime to be a healthy person. Even if it doesn't feel right to do this, I know it's a very normal and acceptable thing to do. The bad feeling is only my OCD and I won't listen to it. I will fight the OCD and the urge to do homework and try to keep my focus on the movie. I am on top of my work, and the only reason I would do work tonight is because of OCD, nothing else."

For Saturday night, William asked his closest friend Mike to go out for pizza and to see a movie. If at any point William felt anxiety, he planned on using mindfulness and calm breathing. He had practiced mindfulness and being attuned to the present moment and planned to use those skills to deal with the situation. He knew that in focusing on the present moment, he would direct his attention to what he was doing, reminding himself that the present was the only moment that was important. Any thoughts about homework were a signal to him that he was not in the present moment, and he would direct his attention back to what he was doing—eating pizza, talking to Mike, or watching the movie. He also planned to use the same self-talk statements that he used for the Friday night exposure. William expected Saturday night to be more challenging for two reasons: He would not have done homework on Friday and he was out with a friend, which meant he was having fun and doing something pleasurable. Therefore, William also planned on doing calm breathing and progressive muscle relaxation during the movie if he felt tense. He also promised himself that he wouldn't disappoint Mike by cancelling and asked his parents to give him extra encouragement to stick with the plan.

Both Jasmine and William benefitted from having a detailed plan of how they would cope with their exposures and any anxiety that they felt in the process. Having a plan made both of them feel more confident and organized about doing the exposures, and they felt like they had a clear idea of what to do with the anxiety when it came up.

Creating a detailed plan also will help you in doing your exposures. When developing your own plan, try to be as specific as possible and also plan for any obstacles that may get in the way of doing your exposure. An example of an obstacle may be having the thought "It's not a big deal to just . . . (straighten your desk, put one thing away, not eat this cookie, do a little homework on Saturday night before I go out)." When OCD minimizes the behavior, it seems easier to do it than not to do it. This is a potential obstacle, and you want to plan for how you will deal with that thought. For example, you might talk back to the OCD and say, "That's right—it's not a big deal either way. Doing homework or not doing homework before I go out won't make a difference in the big picture of school or my grades, but it will make a big difference in overcoming OCD." Therefore, another key part of doing the exposures is challenging your OCD thoughts and beliefs as they come up.

Remember that it's the OCD thoughts and beliefs that usually make kids do the compulsive behaviors like checking, asking, or redoing, and it's these thoughts that cause kids to avoid certain situations. So, when making a plan for each exposure, make sure to include what you will do to challenge your OCD thoughts and beliefs—what will you say in talking back to the OCD? What will your replacement thoughts be like? How will you challenge your OCD beliefs? For example, the *desire for certainty* belief can be challenged by saying back, "I don't need to be certain and don't need to know for sure. There are plenty of times I don't know for sure, and the outcome is fine. Tolerating uncertainty is not only a part of overcoming OCD, but it's a part of life!"

When you have a thinking error, label it as a thinking error and come up with a replacement thought. For example, when Alicia had the thought about getting salmonella poisoning and throwing up, she would tell herself,

> *That is catastrophizing—my favorite thinking error! I won't let thinking errors make the OCD stronger. I can reassure myself that the risk of getting salmonella is very low, but I can also deal with the uncertainty and the possibility that I could get it. I could handle whatever happens. Let me think about what someone without OCD would do in this situation. Probably they would eat the cookies and focus on how good they taste.*

If Alicia does this each time she makes a catastrophizing thinking error, she will eventually stop making them. However, if she doesn't challenge the thought, and instead does the checking and asking behavior, she will continue to make these thinking mistakes, and her OCD will become stronger.

If you find yourself catastrophizing, replace your thoughts with factual information, come up with a neutral way of thinking about the situation, or use it as an opportunity to practice tolerating uncertainty. If you find yourself organized by shoulds, label the shoulds and come up with a replacement thought such as, "It is okay to make mistakes—it makes me human. I will disappoint others, and they will disappoint me. I am still going to have great friends, even though we will all sometimes upset one another." If you find yourself having fusion beliefs, label them as fusion beliefs and replace the thought. For example, say:

> *A thought is just a thought. A thought is not the same as an action. I can have any thought I'd like, and it doesn't mean it will happen. I could think to myself, "I have a million dollars," and it won't mean anything—it doesn't mean that I have a million dollars or will have a million dollars. If it did, then everyone would be a millionaire!*

Remember that when you have OCD, you get stuck in a pattern of thinking too much and overthinking situations. It is easy to get locked in a way of thinking, and thinking, and thinking. Many kids even start to think about their thinking itself! It may be useful to keep in mind the saying, "Don't overthink it!" and simplify what you are doing, much like an observer of your behavior would do. For example, instead of thinking about each move you are making in the bathroom and what you might be touching, how you might be touching it, where the germs are, and what might happen if you get germs on you (a classic pattern of OCD thinking), you could reframe it by saying, "It's just going to the bathroom." Anyone watching you would say, "He's just going to the bathroom." They certainly would not say, "He's getting contaminated with some terminal disease!" (because this is not possible, or else everyone would have diseases because everyone uses bathrooms). By doing this, you are simplifying your thought process, interrupting the OCD train of thought, and using rational self-talk to reduce your anxiety.

Again, by challenging your thoughts when they come up (especially during the exposures), you will break the pattern of thinking this way. You will cause a shift in how you automatically think, and when you pair this with doing exposure/response prevention and facing your fears, you will take control of OCD and return to living anxiety-free!

On the "My Plan" worksheet, or on a separate sheet of paper, write down your plan for the first step on your ladder. Make the plan about what you will do and exactly how you will do it. Try to be as detailed as possible and include all of the ways you can calm your body and challenge your thoughts. Refer to Jasmine and William's plans in this chapter for examples.

My Plan

If you find it hard to do a step on your ladder, consider delaying or disrupting the ritual as a first step. As stated, you can break any step down into smaller steps that are easier to do at first, and then build up to the actual step.

Tolerating Anxiety During Exposures

When doing your exposures, remember that it is important that you also are exposing yourself to the feelings of anxiety itself. The goal is to tolerate the anxiety that naturally comes up, rather than trying to distract yourself from it. When you handle the feelings that arise from the exposures, you improve your ability to handle strong emotions like anxiety in general. Doing this allows you to become less influenced by the anxiety in the big picture.

Using mindfulness to deal with worries and uncomfortable emotions involves being aware of and acknowledging how you are feeling, and being able to accept this as your experience. This acceptance will make worrying easier to deal with and decrease your tendency to react to the worries. It is as simple as saying to yourself, "I am worried right now, and this is what I tend to do at times. I see that I am worrying and that this is causing me to feel uncomfortable in my body and to have a general feeling of uneasiness." Also, mindfulness encourages you to focus on and just *be* in the present moment at hand. In the present moment, you will see that you are okay and that nothing bad is happening to you. Anxious thinking makes you *feel like* something bad is happening, but anxious thinking is not an accurate description of what is happening to you now—it is about your fear of what *might* happen or what *might have* happened. You can also practice mindfulness meditation to become skilled at being in the present moment and suspending your thoughts (for example, being in a thoughtless, relaxed state).

Alicia had a hard time tolerating anxiety during the exposures at first. When she would eat foods as part of her exposure (for example, food from a bake sale or trigger foods like grilled cheese and tomatoes), she would watch television to distract herself and be able to "get through" the exposure. Although this "getting through it" approach technically allowed her to check off steps from her ladder, it didn't allow her to really habituate to them. Alicia distracted herself from the experience of facing her fears and doing the steps on her ladder, so she missed the goal of being able to tolerate the anxiety and discomfort. When I was working with Alicia, we discussed her tendency to focus on TV to deal with the exposures and discussed how she could use mindfulness to stay present in the situation. She then repeated the steps on her ladder without watching TV, and although it was difficult at times, she learned that she could handle the anxiety, and as she did, it would decrease.

Ways to tolerate anxiety during the exposures include mindfulness, calm breathing, and self-talk. For example, when the anxiety comes up, you can recognize it and note that it is there, do calm breathing, and remind yourself that you can handle it and that feeling anxious is not a sign that anything bad will happen. Also, remind yourself that you can handle anything that comes your way. With practice, you will start to change your experience of anxiety, see it for what it is, and not react to it.

If you become panicky during the exposures, it's best to set a time limit and give yourself 5–10 minutes to calm down, and if you don't, then temporarily stop the exposure practice. Once you have calmed down, it's important to try it again as soon as possible. Again, you don't want to give power to the anxiety to cause more avoidance. If you are flooded with anxious thoughts, try writing them down and then going back to the exposure practice. Again, you want to be able to stay with these uncomfortable thoughts and build your muscle for handling them.

Motivating Yourself

The exposure phase is the most important part of overcoming OCD. It is when you apply all of the information that you have learned about OCD, as well as the coping strategies, and decide to take control of OCD. It also is the most challenging part and the one that requires you to be the strongest, most determined, and most confident. You have made a decision to fight your OCD and not let it control your life anymore. Whenever you feel discouraged, try to remember this mindset and also ask for help from a parent if you need it. It is completely normal to find the exposures challenging, but I am 100% certain that if you stick with it and continue to do them, it will get easier and you will feel better.

Remind yourself of the concepts discussed at the end of Chapter 2, including being proactive, being hopeful, and believing in yourself. Use the strategies reviewed in the last section, particularly calm breathing, positive self-talk, replacing thinking errors with balanced thoughts, and using mindfulness, to cope with the exposures.

It is very helpful to reward yourself each time you do an exposure by marking the step on your calendar with either a star sticker or a check (my adult clients use star stickers as well). Seeing your progress visually—as stickers or checks add up—allows you to feel more energized and excited about the great work you are doing. It also highlights how far you are getting in facing your fears and taking control of OCD. This usually makes kids more motivated to move up their ladders!

Finally, here is one more thing to keep in mind, which is very important: **Behavior change happens first; cognitive change happens sec-**

ond. This means that you will be able to change your behavior and take the steps on your ladder *before* you will stop having the OCD thoughts and urges to do the rituals, such as checking. With time, changing your behavior and not doing your typical OCD behaviors and rituals will lead to changes in your thoughts (cognitive changes). Eventually the OCD thoughts will stop.

> **Remember:**
>
> Behavior change happens first; cognitive change happens second.

Taking the First Step

Now that you have finished reading the first eight chapters, it is time to take the first step on your ladder (use the plan you developed earlier). After you have done the first step enough times to be able to do it without feeling anxious, move up to the next step. Continue this process and work toward facing all of the steps on your ladder. The next chapter also is about facing your fears.

What I Know Now

This chapter focused on preparing you to face your fears. The process of exposure/response prevention (ERP) was described in detail, and the theory behind exposure was explained. You learned about habituation and how you can habituate to, or become used to, your OCD situations as you practice them repetitively and frequently and stay in them for a prolonged period of time. You learned how to use your ladder and make detailed plans for your steps, including which strategies you will use to cope with the exposures. The importance of tolerating anxiety and not distracting yourself was discussed. Finally, you read about how to motivate yourself throughout the process.

10

Becoming Resilient to OCD

Going the Extra Mile With Exposures

> "When facing my fears, I used a lot of self-talk. I read my note cards twice a day and ended up memorizing them. I would tell myself that there was only one way to get rid of this OCD and that was to face my fears. When I got to the top and finished my ladder, I realized how much I was able to do and how much I improved."
>
> —Micah, age 9

This chapter expands on Chapter 9 and also focuses on facing your fears. Therefore, this chapter is also about the *behavior* part of OCD. As a review, you have learned about the three parts of OCD and anxiety: body, thoughts, and behavior.

This is the last chapter on the three parts, and the goal is to work toward finishing your ladder after reading this chapter.

Completing Your Ladder

By now, you should have taken at least the first step on your ladder, and it's likely that you also have done additional steps. Hopefully these exposures have gone well and you have learned that by practicing each step and staying in your trigger situations long enough, the anxiety decreases and you are able to habituate to (get used to) the situation. By resisting the urge to do your usual OCD behaviors (like checking, washing, telling, asking, ordering, or redoing), you have challenged the OCD and broken the OCD cycle. Although this process of exposures may have led to an increase in your anxiety level, you are reminding yourself that by tolerating the anxiety that comes during the practices now, you are one step closer to getting rid of anxiety in the long run.

As you continue to move up your ladder and eventually complete all of the steps, it is important to remember the following:

> The three keys to exposures: doing each step *repetitively*, doing each step *frequently*, and staying in each situation for a *prolonged* period of time.
> That you can break down any step into smaller steps to make it easier to practice.
> If really overwhelmed, pause and use the relaxation skills.
> If really overwhelmed, start with delaying or disrupting the ritual.
> To use strategies (such as calm breathing, self-talk, or challenging thinking errors) while doing the exposures.
> Staying with the anxiety that comes up during the exposures (not distracting yourself from it) will allow you to learn how to handle the anxiety and not react to it (by giving in to the urge to do OCD behaviors).

After doing each step once, make sure to put a sticker or a checkmark beside the step. Then, once you have practiced it enough that you no longer get anxious or have a hard time doing it at all, put another sticker or check on the other side of the ladder. Measuring your progress this way is very useful and keeps you motivated and inspired to continue moving up your ladder.

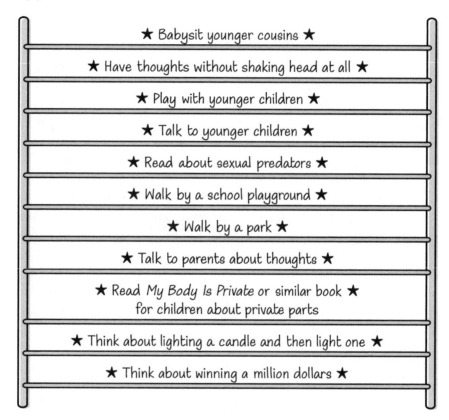

★ Babysit younger cousins ★

★ Have thoughts without shaking head at all ★

★ Play with younger children ★

★ Talk to younger children ★

★ Read about sexual predators ★

★ Walk by a school playground ★

★ Walk by a park ★

★ Talk to parents about thoughts ★

★ Read *My Body Is Private* or similar book ★
for children about private parts

★ Think about lighting a candle and then light one ★

★ Think about winning a million dollars ★

Going the Extra Mile: Pushing Yourself

When doing the exposures, the idea is to begin with easier ones and gradually move up to more challenging ones. In addition, it is best to push yourself to go even further and really go the extra mile in stepping outside of your "comfort zone." Usually, the higher items on your ladder are the ones that will require you to push yourself the most. It's important that you include your hardest exposure on the ladder. Even if you don't think that you can or will do it, it's best to include it. You can always add a few more on the top of your ladder.

comfort zone: refers to what you are comfortable with and comfortable doing; facing your fears involves going outside of your comfort zone

For example, Alicia pushed herself to include drinking milk that expired 2 days earlier at the top of her ladder. This was really effective in getting her over her fears about becoming sick. Once she was able to take this step (which completed her ladder) and realized that nothing bad came from it, she was always able to refer back to this as a good example of how it's not as easy as she thought it was to get sick from drinking milk or eating food. When a situation involving food came up naturally (one that would have previously triggered her OCD), she would remind herself of when she drank "expired" milk and was okay, and then she would be able to eat the food without a problem. Because of her hard work and dedication to completing her ladder, OCD no longer influenced her life or controlled her thoughts. The more that Alicia was able to do this, the less she even had to remind herself of what she had accomplished. In other words, she stopped thinking of the "potential risks" altogether. By getting really good at not giving in and doing OCD behaviors, she caused her OCD thoughts to eventually stop. Gradually, Alicia got to the point where she could be in a situation that would have previously triggered her OCD, and the OCD thoughts didn't come up at all.

It may be that your ladder already includes several steps that involve really pushing yourself. However, if your ladder is lacking in these kinds of steps, it is a good idea to add a few. For example, Alicia also ate chips that had fallen on the floor and ate sushi (raw fish), even though these items weren't on her ladder, because they were ways to really push herself to challenge her OCD. These steps, combined with those at the top of her ladder, such as eating raw cookie dough, represented her most challenging exposures and required her to really push herself. We did these hardest steps together—as I encouraged her to do them (and I also did them with her, although I'm not complaining about having to eat chocolate chip cookie dough during my workday!)—and she did incredibly well.

Although these exposures were hard to do and Alicia worried quite a bit afterward, we talked through it and discussed how these things were fine to do and that people did them all of the time. Each time we did it, it became easier. Alicia challenged her worries and used detached mindfulness to help her recognize that her worries were just thoughts and nothing else (for example, that her worries were not a prediction of what was to come). While we talked about how low the risk was, we also discussed how she had done uncertainty training and was better able to tolerate the uncertainty of the situation. It was fine that she didn't know for sure if it was *completely* safe (just like everything else in life). Alicia reminded herself of other areas in her life that involved uncertainty but didn't trigger her OCD (such as riding her bike, walking her dog, getting shots at the doctor's office, or her parents going on vacation without her). She had to change her thinking, and at times she asked me to reassure her that she wouldn't get sick (it's very common to want this reassurance from others); however, I always asked her to give herself the reassurance *and* reminded her to continue being able to tolerate uncertainty.

Here are some other examples of going the extra mile during exposures:

> using the bathroom without washing your hands at all;
> drinking from a straw that fell on the floor;
> reorganizing your surroundings by turning the clock upside down on the wall, tilting all of the pictures on the wall (in different ways!), wearing mismatched socks to bed, and sleeping with your blanket unevenly upon you—all at once;
> eating food from the floor inside and from the ground outside;
> stepping on lines and cracks while purposely having bad thoughts about family members;
> walking through the halls of a hospital;
> watching videos of people throwing up online; or
> having the thought of harming others and not confessing/telling anyone about it.

Remember that using the imaginal exposure recordings (again, usually recommended for teens ages 15–18) is another way of facing your fears in an extreme way. Hearing your scariest scenarios play out over and over, without acting on them, is another form of exposure/response prevention.

These extreme exposures can be challenging, but they are magical when it comes to overcoming OCD, as once you have done the hardest steps, it becomes much easier to deal with exposures that occur naturally in life. The same is true for the most challenging ladder practices. For example, a client who wouldn't use a utensil in a restaurant if it had moved off the napkin and touched the table had no trouble doing so once she had used a utensil that came from the floor! It creates a shift in perspective that makes the everyday challenges seem way more manageable.

What I Know Now

This chapter was the last one focused on the three parts of anxiety, and it followed the previous chapter, which also was on the behavior part of anxiety. You have already practiced some steps on your ladder, and now it is time to complete it by taking the rest of the steps. You learned about the value and importance of going the extra mile when doing your exposures and pushing yourself to the top of your ladder and beyond. By doing this, you will challenge your OCD even more and become more resilient to OCD.

Stress
Management

"My symptoms always got worse when there were a lot of changes going on, like starting the school year. Exam time was always a trigger, and so was when my parents went out of town. I learned how important it was to keep myself calm and be able to handle my stress better. It wasn't perfect, but it got a lot better."

—Jenny, age 14

Learning how to manage stress is an important component of living a healthy life, and for children and teens with OCD, managing stress is a necessary part of overcoming OCD. Children with OCD consistently report that their OCD symptoms get worse when they are stressed. Anytime you struggle with anxiety and worry, it is a good idea to examine what usually makes you stressed and focus on how you can manage it better. Therefore, this chapter will focus on *stress management*.

Stress Management

Stress is a feeling of tension or nervousness that usually comes from feeling pressure (such as when you have too many things to do), from having to do something unpleasant, or from being disappointed about something (such as when you expected something to happen, but it didn't). Stress usually causes the body to feel restless and uneasy, much like anxiety, but usually on a less intense level. Stress can cause anxiety, and that is why kids with OCD report that stress makes their OCD worse.

> **stress:** a feeling of tension or nervousness that usually comes from feeling pressure, from having to do something unpleasant, or from being disappointed about something

When teaching kids about stress, I use a "beaker" analogy. A beaker measures the amount of stress you have. Normal daily life always has some stress in it: having to be somewhere on time, having to do something that your parents asked you to do, forgetting to hand in your homework, finding out the shirt you planned on wearing is in the wash, and so on. In general, these are "little things" that, although annoying, most kids roll with and don't get overwhelmed by.

If you find yourself overreacting to these little things, then it may indicate that there are other, more significant things causing your beaker level to rise. Examples of more meaningful things that tend to universally cause stress include:

> getting a bad grade in a class,

> having a lot of work and not enough time to complete it,

> social media stress,
> parents fighting (or worse, separating/divorcing),
> moving,
> losing someone you love,
> a pet dying,
> being teased or bullied by other kids, including cyberbullying,
> fighting with friends or siblings,
> being sick or having the flu,
> being undernourished or undereating, and
> sleep deprivation.

Any of these bigger items will cause your beaker level to rise. When your beaker gets too high, it may overflow. When this happens, you may find yourself having a meltdown, crying, screaming, panicking, or acting out in other ways.

Take a moment and consider what things tend to cause you to feel stressed out—whether it's "intermittent" stress, which is short-term stress like getting into an argument with your friend, or "chronic" stress, which is ongoing, such as continually getting overwhelmed by school-work or being in a home where there is a lot of arguing or yelling—and write them down on the "Things That Make Me Stressed Out" worksheet or on a separate sheet of paper.

Things That Make Me Stressed Out:

Only you can manage your beaker and control its level. It is your job to manage stress, and the earlier you learn how to effectively do this, the better off you will be in the long run.

There are two ways of dealing with stress:

1. preventing your beaker level from rising in the first place (prevention), and
2. lowering your beaker level once it has gotten too high or is toward the top (treatment).

Preventing Your Level From Rising

There are four pillars of stress management, which help to keep your beaker level from rising. If you manage these well, you will be protected from getting super stressed out:

1. sleep,
2. eating,
3. exercise, and
4. relaxation and meditation.

Sleep Well. Good sleep hygiene refers to having healthy habits around sleep. These include generally sticking with the same bed time and wake time (even on the weekends), not eating or drinking 2–3 hours before bed, and not going in your bed except to sleep. This means that you should not do homework, read, watch TV, or talk on the phone from bed. If you go to sleep and are tossing and turning for 20 minutes, it's best to get out of bed and do something relatively boring until you feel tired and then get back in bed. Otherwise, your bed might become associated with restlessness, instead of relaxing sleep.

Few kids like to hear about the importance of sleep, especially because many parents are strict about bedtime. It is all for good reason, however, because getting enough sleep has been found to lead to better stress management, better concentration and memory, higher reported happiness levels, and less cravings for sugary foods. The opposite is true for sleep deprivation, which makes it harder to manage your mood, control your irritability level, concentrate, pay attention, and learn new information. It also leads to impulsivity and poor food choices, and hurts your immune system, making it harder to fight off colds and viruses.

It's easy to skimp on sleep, especially as you get older, have more homework and extracurricular activities, and also want to socialize by text or by playing video games. The best thing to do is set a time to turn off all technology (unless you are using it to listen to a relaxation track on one of the apps, in which case you should put it on "do not disturb"), unwind, and get to bed. Many clients I work with use the same relaxation track every night, which becomes associated with calmness and sleep for them. It is very beneficial to do relaxation, calming yoga, or meditation right before bed. Relaxing or meditating before bed will usually result in a better quality of sleep. The goal is not just to sleep enough hours (quantity), but to sleep deeply without getting up in the middle of the night (quality). When you are the one in charge of this, it will work better and you will be more likely to stick with the plan. A good motto to use is *"I've never regretted getting a good night's rest"* and to think about how much you enjoy your sleep and waking up feeling refreshed.

Eat Well. Good eating habits are essential when it comes to managing stress. Research has found that eating a balanced and healthy diet is key when it comes to supporting the body in managing the physical effects of stress. When we are stressed, our adrenal glands release adrenaline and cortisol. The adrenal glands are impacted by blood sugar level. Therefore, foods that support a stable blood sugar level are very important.

A variety of vegetables, fruits, and whole grains makes a healthy diet. As much as possible, it is best to eat "whole" foods: foods that have only themselves as ingredients (for example, an apple is just an apple, nothing else; an almond is just an almond and has no other ingredients). Research suggests that organic foods are healthier, as they don't have pesticides, hormones, or antibiotics in them. This includes organic meats, and the best kind is grass-fed. The fewer the chemicals, the better, so the goal is to avoid "processed" foods.

Processed foods and foods with high fructose corn syrup or partially hydrogenated oils are bad for your health and should be avoided or eaten less often. A good rule of thumb is to eat healthy, clean foods 80% of the time, and chill out and eat less healthfully the other 20% of the time. This works well because when you and your friends socialize, you might like to have pizza or sugary foods. It's normal and totally understandable to eat these foods in moderation (20% of the time). If you are too restrictive, or insist on only eating clean foods, that alone will cause you to be stressed! Once again, it's about finding the right balance and not being harsh with yourself when you eat less healthy foods. When it comes to sugar, when you stop eating it regularly, you will find that you don't crave it as much. Most sodas usually contain high fructose corn syrup, and you should switch to drinking water or naturally flavored carbonated beverages that are refreshing and don't contain sugar.

Green tea is a powerful antioxidant, which means it helps your body stay healthy. Other good antioxidants include organic strawberries, blueberries, asparagus, broccoli, and dark green leafy vegetables (organic spinach, kale, etc.). Try to eat colorful vegetables and fruits. You may have heard that's it's great to "eat the rainbow," which means including many different colored fruits and vegetables on your plate. Finally, flax seed can be added to yogurt or cereal, and it is one of the most powerful antioxidants available (you can buy ground flax seed in most healthy grocery stores). In addition to antioxidants, try to eat foods that have a lot of fiber. Talk to your parents about adding these kinds of foods into your regular family meals. It only takes one family member to inspire the entire family to eat better—why not be that person?

> **antioxidant:** a substance naturally found in food and some teas that has been shown to help your body stay healthy

Also, it is very important to drink enough water. Anytime you feel thirsty, this means that your body is already dehydrated. Try to drink two full glasses of water before leaving the house in the morning, and this will get you on the right track. The goal is 8–10 glasses a day—more if you drink caffeine or play a lot of sports.

The Resources section has a list of books for your parents, including some on healthy eating and healthy lifestyles. In addition to the foods listed previously, the "Healthy Foods" chart is a list of foods that support your body's health and ability to manage stress:

Healthy Foods

Almonds	Cherries	Pecans
Apples	Chickpeas	Pineapple
Apricots	Eggs (organic, pasture-raised with omega-3)	Plums
Avocados	Garlic	Poultry

Healthy Foods, continued

Beans (navy, great northern, butter)	Grapes	Seeds (sunflower, sesame)
Beets	Grass-fed beef	Sweet potatoes
Berries	Kiwi	Walnuts
Brown rice pasta	Lentils	Watermelon
Cabbage	Oranges	Wild-caught fish (salmon, halibut, sea bass)
Cashews	Peaches	
Cauliflower	Pears	

I know that all of this healthy advice might seem like something you don't need to do or don't want to do, or like something your parents should hear instead, and so on. All I can say is that I assure you, if you eat healthfully, you will feel better, sleep better, have more energy, have improved concentration and focus, and most of all, be better able to manage your stress and anxiety. You have nothing to lose in making this positive change in how you treat your body—and the earlier your start in life, the better! A good motto is *"I've never regretted eating a healthy meal."*

Exercise. Staying active and exercising regularly is not only important for your health, but also super important in helping you manage stress. Exercise releases tension, and people feel less stressed after they exercise. It also helps to manage your mood and be less irritable. My best advice is to find a sport or activity that you enjoy, such as running, swimming, or karate, and make the time to do it regularly. Once exercise becomes part of your routine, you will see the way it helps you deal with stress and tension. When you have OCD, you need to be even more determined to make exercise a regular activity. In fact, you can even use exercise as a way of getting rid of the anxiety you feel during exposures (for example, "walk off" the anxiety by going on a 30-minute walk until you feel relieved and calmer). A good motto is *"I've never regretted a workout!"*

Practice Relaxation. Even when you are not doing exposures, and even when you are finished with this program, make relaxation a part of your life. Try to consider it a part of your general well-being and healthy lifestyle. Make it part of your bedtime routine to do 10–20 minutes of relaxation before bed, take a weekly yoga class, or do calm breathing throughout your school day. Whichever type of relaxation works best for you should be integrated into your normal daily routine. The more often you practice, the more often you will be relaxed. This means the *less* often you will feel stressed or anxious!

Recently, there has been a lot of focus on being connected with nature and spending time outdoors, and how beneficial this is for emotional and mental health, especially in light of cell phones and technology, which often keep us indoors and can cause stress. Being in nature encourages more creativity and intelligence, and it allows you to get out of your head and your thoughts and more into your surroundings. A good goal would be to find a time each day to be outdoors and off any screens for an hour a day. You could read outside, or go for a walk or run, or just sit and look up at the trees. This promotes a feeling of calm and connection with the Earth.

Express Your Feelings Appropriately. First, it is important to have several people—a few friends and a few adults—with whom you can really open up and talk about your feelings. Often, kids feel that they can talk to at least one of their parents, and I encourage all kids with OCD to talk to their parents about what it feels like to struggle with OCD. It can be hard for parents, siblings, or friends to understand what you are going through and what your experience is like, but don't let that stop you from trying to explain it to them. Even saying something like "The OCD is a constant focus. No matter what I'm doing at the time, OCD is there in the background. I'm working to be free from OCD, but it's caused me a lot of stress and has taken a lot of my time and energy. It helps for others to understand just how hard it is to have OCD" can be helpful. Second, it also is important that you find healthy ways to express your feelings even when someone isn't there to listen. For example, writing in a journal and drawing/painting are appropriate ways to express how you feel.

Self-compassion is when you show kindness and are understanding with yourself. The research on self-compassion is clear: When you are working toward a goal, if you show self-kindness, rather than self-criticism (when you are harsh and judging with yourself), you will be better able to meet your goal. So, whether it's about general stress, or more specifically related to when your OCD gets bad or the exposure practices are not going smoothly, it's at those times when you need to show the most self-compassion.

Stay on Top of Things. One of the best ways to prevent getting overwhelmed and stressed is to stay on top of things, mainly your school-work and larger school-related projects. It is very stressful when you get behind. If you have a lot to do, make a list and check it off as things get done. Keeping your room clean and staying on top of chores and responsibilities at home also can help you feel organized. It can be easy to fall behind, and many kids struggle with procrastination. Procrastinators wait until they feel motivated to do something to do it. Non-procrastinators just do it and take action, regardless of how they feel. This is the same thing as being proactive. Thus, being proactive is another way to prevent getting stressed out.

Finally, people are more productive and effective when their busy schedule is balanced out by down time and free time. This is referred to as "work-life balance." I recommend having one day a week that is free of obligations, including scheduled activities and homework. Everyone needs to have a day when they can relax and have fun. These days allow you to reset and also allow you to be creative and imaginative (when everything is planned for us, we tend not to be very creative). Creative freedom also can help you feel de-stressed! Ironically, taking the time to have this one free day a week will make you more productive and better at getting your work done the other 6 days. As mentioned previously, making sure you have time away from screens is essential when it comes to feeling balanced.

Put Things in Perspective. When there is a lot on your plate, try to put things in perspective. It is easy to lose perspective, and when you do, you get out of touch with how easily things can be done. Even if there is a lot to do, you have likely had times like this in the past and worked through it all just fine. It also can help to realize that no matter how bad it gets, there also are many things that are going right. Try to keep a balanced perspective and be mindful of what is going well. The goal is to stay focused on one thing at a time (without multitasking). Stay focused only on the one task in front of you, without thinking about everything else you have to do.

Minimize Your News Exposure. Watching the news can be very depressing—and also unnecessarily alarming! Remember that the news has the goal of reporting what is wrong in the world, including terrible and shocking stories. In fact, the news stations are drawn to terrible events and thrive on reporting them. You never turn on the news to see stories of people being kind to one another, kids who had a great vacation with their family, people doing a great job at work, all of the thousands of safe flights that happened that day, and so on.

Whether you watch it or not, the news is reporting bad stuff. When you have OCD, you are dealing with enough stress, so limiting the news is an easy way to reduce the stress you are exposed to. Try to avoid it as much as you can, and if you feel like you are missing out on the world's events, ask one of your parents or teachers to give you a brief summary of two or three big stories that are not terrible or shocking.

Treating a Full Beaker

Sometimes, you either fall behind on keeping up with prevention strategies like sleeping well, eating well, and exercising or, despite doing these things, a stressor is so intense that you get overwhelmed and your beaker level rises. It could be that your OCD flares and you are completely overwhelmed. When this happens, you may find that the only thing that you *can* do is work on lowering the level! Here are some ideas:

1. Exercise: Go for a long walk or a run, do 100 jumping jacks or push-ups, or do a handstand against the wall until you feel physically tired.
2. Take a bubble bath (you can add relaxing music or read a magazine) or a hot shower.
3. Distract yourself—read a book, watch TV or a movie, or use the ABCs to make lists.
4. Journal about what is upsetting you: Make a list of everything that is causing you to be upset and stressed.
5. Give yourself a time out from whatever you are doing and focus on restoring your sense of well-being.
6. Play an instrument.
7. Play with a pet.
8. Cry. Just let it out.
9. Get out of the house. Ask your parent to take you somewhere to break up the routine or go for a walk.
10. Do every relaxation strategy until you calm down: calm breathing, PMR, imagery, mindfulness meditation, and yoga.

This list is just a sample of what you could do. You are an expert on yourself and know what works best for you. Using the "I Can Lower My Beaker Level By" worksheet, or a separate sheet of paper, write down what you can do to lower your beaker level once it has become full.

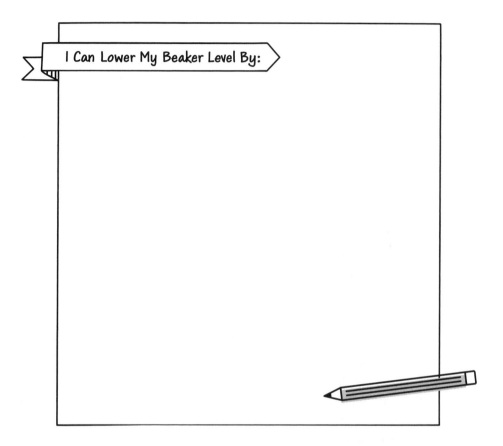

I Can Lower My Beaker Level By:

Positive Self-Talk and Positive Thinking

Being positive and having a positive outlook on life is a great way to generally stay unstressed. A positive attitude also will be valuable to you during times when you do get stressed out. Sometimes, it can be easy to complain, be negative, and focus on what didn't work out well. In fact, many kids get stuck in thinking about the negative or what is not perfect. It is possible to shift this to a different outlook. It is possible to train yourself to be a more positive, grateful person. With practice, you can develop a more positive attitude.

Here are some tips for being more positive:

1. When you are feeling upset, try to **identify the one specific thing that is upsetting to you**, rather than focusing on the many things that could be upsetting. Many times, people "globalize," meaning that they feel like everything is bad, and focus on all of the things that are not working out for them. This globaliz-

ing tends to make people feel worse and like there is no solution because there are so many problems. Instead, be *specific* about what is upsetting you. This way, you will be able to come up with possible solutions.

2. Recognize that when things go wrong or when you have a lot of work to do, it is a **temporary situation**. It's easy to feel like there is no end in sight or that things won't ever get better, but when you think this way—and see problems as permanent or never going away—your anxiety level increases, and you are more likely to feel unhappy.

3. Ask yourself, "**If I had to say what was positive** in my life right now, what would it be?" and "How would someone who wasn't complaining describe this situation?" Use the answers for your replacement thoughts.

4. Keep a **gratitude journal**. Each day, write down at least two things that went well that day or that you are grateful for. For example, you can write that you are grateful to have such a loving family, that you ate your favorite breakfast, that your teacher forgot to collect the homework you hadn't finished, that your dog cuddled up with you last night, or that you and your friends laughed at lunch. It can be anything big or small, and actually a combination of both is the best because that will help you realize the big things and little things that you are grateful for. Research has found that doing a gratitude practice, such as keeping a gratitude journal, causes people to feel happier overall. It is a fairly simple thing to do—just write in a journal right before falling asleep. The opposite of gratitude is deprivation: When you feel deprivation, your focus is on whatever did not go well, whatever you did not get, or how others have it better than you do. These social comparisons will only make you feel badly. The goal is to focus on what you do have, what is right about you and your life, and what is going well.

5. Be your **biggest fan** and cheer yourself on! Many kids feel down on themselves when times are tough, and these times call for a good amount of self-love and self-compassion. When you are kind to yourself, your self-talk will be positive and supportive. Imagine what you would tell a friend if they were stressed, and then tell it to yourself. Be gentle and understanding with yourself, and compliment yourself, pointing out all that you are doing

right now. Good self-esteem means that you appreciate yourself and still know your strengths, even when you fail.

gratitude journal: a journal in which you write down at least three things that went well each day or that you are grateful for

Developing Your Stress Management Plan

Using the information in this chapter, develop your own stress management plan. List things that you could be doing differently (such as getting 30 more minutes of sleep each night, exercising more often, or eating fruit as a snack) that will help you prevent stress, and then list what you will do if you become stressed and overwhelmed (such as doing jumping jacks, playing the guitar, or taking a bath). Also include what you can do or say to yourself to have a more positive attitude (for example, "When I have a lot of work to do, I will assure myself that it will all get done if I just take one subject at a time and keep my cool"). The "My Stress Management Plan" worksheet includes some space for you to write your own stress management plan.

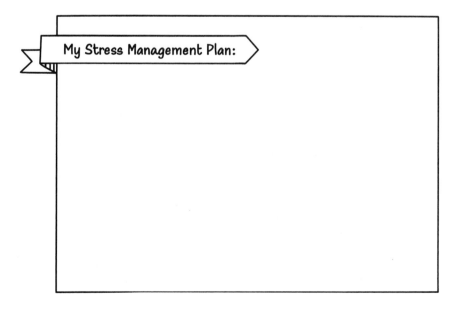

My Stress Management Plan:

What I Know Now

This chapter focused on stress management. The importance of taking a preventative approach to not getting stressed out was discussed, and you learned about sleeping well, eating well, exercising, and other ways to keep your beaker level low. Ideas for what you can do if you do become stressed and overwhelmed were reviewed, including taking a run around the block, journaling your feelings, and distracting yourself. You learned about having a positive attitude and what you can do to have one (such as keeping a gratitude journal). Finally, you developed your own stress management plan.

Congratulations!

Celebrate Yourself and Your Accomplishments

"My family is so proud of me and how far I got and how I overcame my anxiety. Dr. Zucker helped me get over my fears and emotions, and now my life is so much better and easier. I know how hard I worked and am also proud of myself."

—Jonathan, age 9

Congratulations! You made it!

I wish I could be there in person to tell you how *proud* I am of you for reading this book and doing all of the work involved in taking control of OCD. I hope that you and your family can plan a celebration in honor of you and your accomplishments. Many kids and their families have a special meal together or plan a fun activity to celebrate. Whatever works for you and your family is up to you, but there should be some time dedicated to celebrating you and all you have done!

For those who didn't finish your ladder or didn't do every part of the book: The fact that you read it means that you have begun the process of challenging your OCD, and this is something to be proud of. Remember, many kids never end up dealing with their OCD and end up living with it. You may need a little more time, or you may need to get a little older, before fully completing your ladder and engaging in the exposure process. For some, it takes a little longer. The point is to not give up and to keep pushing forward, no matter how small the step or how long it takes.

Celebrating Yourself

As a cognitive-behavior therapist, I am definitely into rewarding yourself. This doesn't necessarily mean buying something for yourself, but it could be about receiving a meaningful trinket or certificate (your parents can download one on a computer) that can be framed. Everyone is different, so everyone will vary on how they want to celebrate this great accomplishment. Most of the time, it is rewarding enough just to have a completed ladder. Several children I have worked with hung up their completed ladders in their rooms. Some have even asked me to shred it as a way of showing their mastery of their OCD. My recommendation is for you to keep the completed ladder, or at least a photo of it, to symbolize your achievement and be a reminder of what you were able to do. Keeping it or a photo of it would also be useful in case OCD symptoms came back in the future.

Most important of all, however, is the message you give yourself about challenging your OCD. It is very important for you to recognize that by completing this program, you have taught yourself the value of working through a problem and tackling it in a straightforward, step-by-step manner. Knowing that it is within your power to overcome an obstacle and deal with a problem is part of being *resilient*. Resilience is the ability to withstand obstacles and bounce back after having bumps in the road. Being confident about your ability to work through problems is a sign of resilience, and after working through your OCD, you deserve to have this confidence!

resilience: the ability to withstand obstacles and bounce back after having bumps in the road

Write down your ideas for celebrating yourself and your accomplishments on the "Ideas for Celebrating" worksheet. What will you do? Who will be included in the celebration? Talk about the plan with your parent(s).

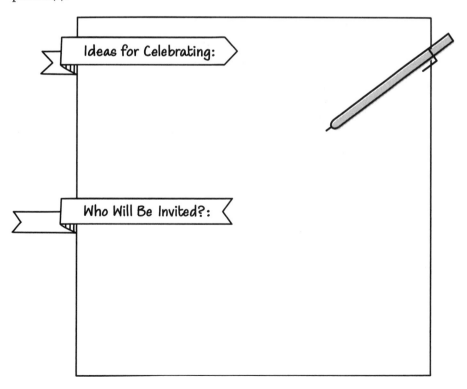

Ideas for Celebrating:

Who Will Be Invited?:

Celebrating Your Accomplishments and All You Have Learned

Reading this book provided you with a lot of information on OCD—what it is and how you take control of it. To summarize, you learned that OCD involves obsessions or compulsions, or both, that the person continues to have despite trying to stop. Common types of obsessions and compulsions were listed, and hopefully your particular type was mentioned. You learned about the OCD cycle (event-thought-feeling-action) and the three parts of OCD: body, thoughts, and behavior.

To address the **body** part, you learned calm breathing, PMR, imagery, mindfulness meditation, and some yoga moves. To address the **thoughts** part, you learned how to master your worries, tolerate uncertainty, use loops and imaginal exposure recordings, identify and replace thinking errors, and use mindfulness, including detached mindfulness. To address the **behavior** part, you learned about exposure/response prevention (ERP) and the importance of facing your fears. Medication options also were reviewed.

After creating your ladder, you used ERP to take each step and face your fears. You also learned about pushing yourself when facing your fears to get to the top of your ladder and even beyond. Other conditions that may occur at the same time as OCD were reviewed. Finally, you learned about the importance of managing stress and what you can do to keep your stress level (or beaker level) low, which is particularly useful because OCD can get worse when stress levels rise.

Wow! You have learned *a lot*! Some of these lessons, such as calm breathing, mastering worries, tolerating uncertainty, and knowing how to manage stress, will be useful for you later in life. Therefore, continuing to practice and use these strategies can become part of how you live your life. In addition, they will help you if your OCD symptoms come up again.

Preventing OCD From Coming Back and What to Do if It Returns

There is still a lot that psychologists and psychiatrists need to figure out about OCD. One of the things we do know is that sometimes OCD comes back, even for no apparent reason. Much of the time there is a trigger to it (like stress), but sometimes there is not. For some children, once they overcome OCD, it may never be a big issue again. For others, however, it may come and go. If this happens, there is nothing to feel bad about. Most of the time, the same symptoms appear, but sometimes the symptoms shift to other themes or worries. Either way, the same treatment approach applies, and that is the most important thing to keep in mind.

The best advice to try to prevent OCD symptoms from coming back is to continue to do exposures as a regular part of life. You want to keep facing your fears, ensure that you don't avoid situations, and look for opportunities to face triggering situations as much as you can. Remember that the goal is to adopt an exposure lifestyle. By doing this, you will make it harder for OCD to become a problem again. Also, managing stress is essential when it comes to relapse prevention.

If OCD symptoms return, continue to confront OCD and deal with it in the way that you have been while using this program. The same approach will be useful no matter what symptoms of OCD come up and no matter how small or how big an interference they cause. Regardless of the severity of the OCD symptoms, the CBT approach, using ERP, is the most effective. Now that you know it so well and have mastered it, you can apply it again in the future if needed.

Knowing how to deal with OCD is the best defense. It's sort of like if you had allergies: You may get successfully treated and never have symptoms again, or you may have symptoms again at another point in your life. The point is that you have an effective method of dealing with it, and you know how to use this method again should you need to.

If OCD comes back, try not to get too upset about the fact that it returned. Instead, get geared up to face your symptoms and work through it just as you already have. You've done it once, and you can do it again. Try to remember your success and what in particular worked best for you. If it returns, it will be important to remember what strategies and approaches were most effective for you. Thus, take a moment to write down which of the techniques helped you the most and which were most useful for you (you can refer to the beginning of Chapter 9 for a comprehensive list of what you learned). Use the "Techniques That Helped Me the Most" worksheet or a separate sheet of paper.

Techniques That Helped Me the Most:

What I Know Now

This chapter focused on celebrating yourself and all that you have accomplished by completing this program and taking control of OCD. The value of seeing the process of tackling a problem and knowing that it was within your abilities to solve it was discussed. There was a review of all you have learned and done, and what worked best for you. Finally, tips on preventing OCD from coming back were reviewed. In particular, having an exposure lifestyle and making exposure part of your regular life was emphasized.

Conclusion
Best Wishes for Continued Success

Congratulations again on completing this book and working through the program. By now you should feel very proud of your accomplishments, and you should be experiencing the rewards of working so hard to *take control of OCD*! Continue to refer back to this book from time to time as a refresher on what facing OCD was like and what specifically was most useful for you. Managing your stress level and continuing to challenge any thinking mistakes that may come up will help strengthen your psychological well-being.

I wish you all the best for the future. I hope you experience the freedom that comes from managing OCD well, and I hope you feel confident about your determination in facing your fears and overcoming them. Best of luck in all that you do!

Best wishes,

Dr. Bonnie Zucker

Resources

Recommended Books for Parents and Professionals

Obsessive-Compulsive Disorder

Abramowitz, J. S. (2018). *Getting over OCD: A 10-step workbook for taking back your life* (2nd ed.). The Guilford Press.

Hershfield, J. (2015). *When a family member has OCD: Mindfulness and cognitive behavioral skills to help families affected by obsessive-compulsive disorder*. New Harbinger.

Hyman, B. M., & Pedrick, C. (2010). *The OCD workbook: Your guide to breaking free from obsessive-compulsive disorder* (3rd ed.). New Harbinger.

McKenney, K., Simpson, A., & Stewart, S. E. (2020). *OCD in children and adolescents: The "OCD is not the boss of me" manual*. The Guilford Press.

Zucker, B. (2017). *Parenting kids with OCD: A guide to understanding and supporting your child with OCD*. Prufrock Press.

General Anxiety

Leahy, R. L. (2006). *The worry cure: Seven steps to stop worry from stopping you*. Harmony Books.

Wells, A. (2009). *Metacognitive therapy for anxiety and depression*. The Guilford Press.

Wilson, R., & Lyons, L. (2013). *Anxious kids, anxious parents: 7 ways to stop the worry cycle and raise courageous and independent children*. Health Communications.

Zucker, B. (2016). *Anxiety-free kids: An interactive guide for parents and children* (2nd ed.). Prufrock Press.

Social Anxiety

Antony, M. M., & Swinson, R. P. (2017). *The shyness and social anxiety workbook: Proven step-by-step techniques for overcoming your fear* (3rd ed.). New Harbinger.

Perfectionism

Antony, M. M., & Swinson, R. P. (2009). *When perfect isn't good enough: Strategies for coping with perfectionism* (2nd ed.). New Harbinger.

Braiker, H. B. (2002). *The disease to please: Curing the people-pleasing syndrome*. McGraw-Hill.

Panic Attacks

Wilson, R. (2019). *Facing panic: Self-help for people with panic attacks* (2nd ed.). Anxiety Disorders Association of America.

Health Anxiety

Taylor, S., & Asmundson, G. J. G. (2004). *Treating health anxiety: A cognitive-behavioral approach*. The Guilford Press.

Hair Pulling

Keuthen, N. J., Stein, D. J., & Christenson, G. A. (2001). *Help for hair pullers: Understanding and coping with trichotillomania*. New Harbinger.

Mouton-Odum, S., & Golomb, R. G. G. (2013). *A parent guide to hair pulling disorder: Effective parenting strategies for children with trichotillomania*. Goldum.

Pentzel, F. (2003). *The hair-pulling problem: A complete guide to trichotillomania*. Oxford University Press.

Health/Nutrition

Lipman, F. (2019). *How to be well: The 6 keys to a happy and healthy life*. Houghton Mifflin Harcourt.

Longo, V. (2018). *The longevity diet: Discover the new science behind stem cell activation and regeneration to slow aging, fight disease, and optimize weight*. Penguin Random House.

NurrieStearns, M., & NurrieStearns, R. (2010). *Yoga for anxiety: Meditations and practices for calming the body and mind*. New Harbinger.

Robbins, J. (2006). *Healthy at 100: The scientifically proven secrets of the world's healthiest and longest-lived peoples*. Ballantine Books.

Singer, M. A. (2007). *The untethered soul: The journey beyond yourself*. New Harbinger.

Weintraub, A. (2004). *Yoga for depression: A compassionate guide to relieve suffering through yoga*. Broadway Books.

Positive Parenting

Dweck, C. S. (2016). *Mindset: The new psychology of success*. Ballantine Books. (Original work published 2006)

Hall, K. D., & Cook, M. H. (2011). *The power of validation: Arming your child against bullying, peer pressure, addiction, self-harm, and out-of-control emotions*. New Harbinger.

Hallowell, E. M. (2002). *The childhood roots of adult happiness: Five steps to help kids create and sustain lifelong joy*. Ballantine Books.

Seligman, M. E. P. (2007). *The optimistic child: A proven program to safeguard children against depression and build lifelong resilience*. Houghton Mifflin.

Stixrud, W., & Johnson, N. (2018). *The self-driven child: The science and sense of giving your kids more control over their lives.* Viking.

Recommended Books for Children and Teens

Alvord, M. K., & McGrath, A. (2017). *Conquer negative thinking for teens: A workbook to break the nine thought habits that are holding you back.* New Harbinger.

Covey, S. (2014). *The 7 habits of highly effective teens.* Touchstone.

Flanagan Burns, E. (2014). *Ten turtles on Tuesday: A story for children about obsessive-compulsive disorder.* Magination Press.

Golomb, R. G., & Vavrichek, S. M. (2019). *The hair pulling "habit" and you: How to solve the trichotillomania puzzle* (Rev. ed.). Writers Cooperative of Greater Washington.

Guber, T. & Kalish, L. (2005). *Yoga pretzels: 50 fun activities for kids and grownups.* Barefoot Books.

Huebner, D. (2007). *What to do when your brain gets stuck: A kid's guide to overcoming OCD.* Magination Press.

Wagner, A. P. (2013). *Up and down the worry hill: A children's book about obsessive-compulsive disorder and its treatment* (3rd ed.). Lighthouse Press.

Zucker, B. (2016). *Anxiety-free kids: An interactive guide for parents and children* (2nd ed.). Prufrock Press.

Recommended CDs

Alvord, M., Zucker, B., & Alvord, B. (2011). *Relaxation and self-regulation techniques for children and teens: Mastering the mind-body connection* [Audio CD]. Research Press.

Lite, L. (2006). *Indigo dreams: 4 children's stories designed to decrease stress and anxiety while increasing self-esteem and awareness* [Audio CD]. Lite Books.

Recommended Apps

> Calm
> CBT Tools for Youth
> Headspace
> Insight Timer
> iSleep Easy

Organizations

American Psychological Association (APA)
Washington, DC
https://www.apa.org

Anxiety and Depression Association of America (ADAA)
Silver Spring, MD
https://adaa.org

Association for Behavioral and Cognitive Therapies (ABCT)
New York, NY
https://www.abct.org

National Alliance on Mental Illness (NAMI)
Arlington, VA
https://www.nami.org

National Institute of Mental Health (NIMH)
Bethesda, MD
https://www.nimh.nih.gov

International OCD Foundation (IOCDF)
Boston, MA
https://iocdf.org

The TLC Foundation for Body-Focused Repetitive Behaviors
Santa Cruz, CA
https://www.bfrb.org

Inpatient and Day Treatment Programs Specifically for OCD

This list is not exhaustive. For a more expansive list, visit https://iocdf.org.

The Gateway Institute
Scottsdale, AZ
https://www.gatewayocd.com

McLean OCD Institute
Houston, TX
http://houstonocdprogram.org

Louisville OCD Clinic
Louisville, KY
https://louisvilleocdclinic.com

McLean Hospital OCD Institute
Belmont, MA
https://www.mcleanhospital.org/ocd

Mount Sinai Obsessive-Compulsive and Related Disorders Program
New York, NY
https://www.mountsinai.org

OCD & Anxiety Program of Southern California
Santa Monica, CA
https://socalocdprogram.org

The OCD & Anxiety Treatment Center
Bountiful, UT
https://www.theocdandanxietytreatmentcenter.com

The OCD Clinics
New Braunfels, TX
https://theocdclinics.com

The OCD Program at Linder Center of HOPE
Mason, OH
https://lindnercenterofhope.org

Pediatric Psychology Associates' Anxiety and OCD Intensive Outpatient Program
Aventura, FL
https://www.southfloridatherapists.com/anxiety-and-ocd-intensive-out
patient-program-iop-treatment-option

Psychological Care & Healing (PCH) OCD and Anxiety Clinic
Los Angeles, CA
https://www.pchtreatment.com

Rogers Behavioral Health OCD Center
Oconomowoc, WI
https://rogersbh.org

UCLA Child OCD Intensive Treatment Program
Los Angeles, CA
https://www.semel.ucla.edu/catp/child-ocd-intensive-treatment-program

Weill Cornell Psychiatry Specialty Center
New York, NY
https://weillcornell.org/services/psychiatry/weill-cornell-psychiatry-
specialty-center

References

Abramowitz, J. S. (2018). *Getting over OCD: A 10-step workbook for taking back your life* (2nd ed.). The Guilford Press.

Albert, U., Bogetto, F., Maina, G., Saracco, P., Brunatto, C., & Mataix-Cols, D. (2010). Family accommodation in obsessive-compulsive disorder: Relation to symptom dimensions, clinical and family characteristics. *Psychology Research, 179*(2), 204–211. https://doi.org/10.1016/j.psychres.2009.06.008

American Psychiatric Association. (2013). *Diagnostic and statistical manual of mental disorders* (5th ed.). https://doi.org/10.1176/appi.books.9780890425596

Antony, M. M., & Swinson, R. P. (2017). *The shyness and social anxiety workbook: Proven techniques for overcoming your fears* (3rd ed.). New Harbinger.

Boileau, B. (2011). A review of obsessive-compulsive disorder in children and adolescents. *Dialogues in Clinical Neuroscience, 13*(4), 401–411. https://doi.org/10.31887/dcns.2011.13.4/bboileau

Brantley, J. (2007). *Calming your anxious mind: How mindfulness and compassion can free you from anxiety, fear, and panic* (2nd ed.). New Harbinger.

Covey, S. R. (2004). *The 7 habits of highly effective people: Powerful lessons in personal change.* Free Press.

Flament, M. F., Whitaker, A., Rapoport, J. L., Davies, M., Berg, C. Z., Kalikow, K., Sceery, W., & Shaffer, D. (1988). Obsessive compulsive disorder in adolescence: An epidemiological study. *Journal of the American Academy of Child & Adolescent Psychiatry, 27*(6), 764–771. https://doi.org/10.1097/00004583-198811000-00018

Hershfield, J. (2015). *When a family member has OCD: Mindfulness and cognitive behavioral skills to help families affected by obsessive-compulsive disorder.* New Harbinger.

Hollon, S. D., Stewart, M. O., & Strunk, D. (2006). Enduring effects for cognitive-behavior therapy in the treatment of depression and anxiety. *Annual Review of Psychology, 57,* 285–315. https://doi.org/10.1146/annurev.psych.57.102904.190044

Hyman, B. M., & Pedrick, C. (2010). *The OCD workbook: Your guide to breaking free from obsessive-compulsive disorder* (3rd ed.). New Harbinger.

Hyman, M. (2014). *The blood sugar solution: The ultrahealthy program for losing weight, preventing disease, and feeling great now.* Little, Brown Spark.

Leahy, R. L. (2006). *The worry cure: Seven steps to stop worry from stopping you.* Harmony Books.

McKenney, K., Simpson, A., & Stewart, S. E. (2020). *OCD in children and adolescents: The "OCD is not the boss of me" manual.* The Guilford Press.

Neff, K. (2015). *Self-compassion: The proven power of being kind to yourself.* Morrow.

Oliver, G., Dean, O., Camfield, D., Blair-West, S., Ng, C., Berk, M., & Sarris, J. (2015). N-Acetyl Cysteine in the treatment of obsessive compulsive and related disorders: A systematic review. *Clinical Psychopharmacology and Neuroscience, 13*(1), 12–24. https://doi.org/10.9758/cpn.2015.13.1.12

The Pediatric OCD Treatment Study Team. (2004). Cognitive-behavioral therapy, sertraline, and their combination for children and adolescents with obsessive-compulsive disorder: The POTS randomized controlled trial. *Journal of the American Medical Association, 292*(16), 1968–1976. https://doi.org/10.1001/jama.292.16.1969

Sigra, S., Hesselmark, E., & Bejerot, S., (2018). Treatment of PANDAS and PANS: A systematic review. *Neuroscience Biobehavioral Reviews, 86,* 51–65. https://doi.org/10.1016/j.neubiorev.2018.01.001

Swedo, S. E., Rapoport, J. L., Leonard, H., Lenane, M. C., & Cheslow, D. L. (1989). Obsessive-compulsive disorder in children and adolescents: Clinical phenomenology of 70 consecutive cases. *Archives of General Psychiatry, 46*(4), 335–341. https://doi.org/10.1001/archpsyc.1989.01810040041007

Walkup, J. T., Albano, A. M., Piacentini, J., Birmaher, B., Compton, S. N., Sherrill, J. T., Ginsburg, G. S., Rynn, M. A., McCracken, J., Waslick, B., Iyengar, S., March, J. S., & Kendall, P. C. (2008). Cognitive behavioral therapy, sertraline, or a combination in childhood anxiety. *New England Journal of Medicine, 359,* 2753–2766. https://doi.org/10.1056/NEJMoa0804633

Wells, A. (2009). *Metacognitive therapy for anxiety and depression.* The Guilford Press.

Wilens, T. E. (2016). *Straight talk about psychiatric medications for kids* (4th ed.). The Guilford Press.

Author's Note: These references were used as resources for various information and suggestions included in this book.

About the Author

Bonnie Zucker, Psy.D., is a licensed psychologist with a background and expertise in psychotherapy with children, adolescents, and adults. She received her doctoral degree in clinical psychology from Illinois School of Professional Psychology in Chicago, her master's degree in applied psychology from University of Baltimore, and her bachelor's degree in psychology from The George Washington University.

Dr. Zucker specializes in the treatment of childhood anxiety disorders and OCD. Using a cognitive-behavioral therapy (CBT) approach, she has helped hundreds of children overcome their OCD by teaching them coping skills, methods for challenging their faulty thinking, and doing exposure/response prevention (ERP). Dr. Zucker also works with parents to guide them in how to best respond to their child's OCD and anxiety.

Dr. Zucker is the director of Bonnie Zucker & Associates in Rockville, MD, a private practice group. She was named one of *Washingtonian* magazine's top therapists in several fields, including CBT, OCD, and phobias. In addition to being active in training mental health professionals on the treatment of anxiety disorders and OCD, Dr. Zucker wrote *Anxiety-Free Kids: An Interactive Guide for Parents and Children* (2nd ed.), *Parenting Kids With OCD: A Guide to Understanding and Supporting Your Child With OCD*, and *Something Very Sad Happened: A Toddler's Guide to Understanding Death*. She also coauthored *Resilience Builder Program for Children and Adolescents: Enhancing Social Competence and Self-Regulation (A Cognitive-Behavioral Group Approach)*, *Relaxation and Self-Regulation Techniques for Children and Teens: Mastering the Mind-Body Connection* (Audio CD), and *Relaxation and Wellness Techniques: Mastering the Mind-Body Connection* (Audio CD).